Alchemy of the Heart:
Shavon Sun Cloud

By
L. Neil Thrussell

Copyright © 2023 by L. Neil Thrussell

All rights reserved, including the right to reproduce this work in any form whatsoever, without permission in writing from the publisher, except for brief passages in connection with a review.

Published by *Best U Can B Inc.*
www.bestucanb.ca

Title: Alchemy of the Heart: Shavon Sun Cloud
Format: Electronic book (English)
This publication has been assigned: 978-1-988417-02-8
Format: Paperback book (English)
This publication has been assigned: 978-1-988417-01-1
Format: Hardcover book (English)
This publication has been assigned: 978-1-988417-18-9

Forthcoming books also by L. Neil Thrussell
Title: Alquimia del Corazón : Nube del sol de Shavon
Format: Electronic book (Spanish)
This publication has been assigned: 978-1-988417-17-2
Format: Paperback book (Spanish)
This publication has been assigned: 978-1-988417-16-5

Editing: Tina Thrussell
Book cover: L. Neil Thrussell
Cover Image: Under licensed use from Dreamstime LLC

Acknowledgements

I would like to thank my friend, Karen Christine Angermayer, who graciously put me in touch with a plethora of Irish Shamans to help me in the research for this book. Your offer, Karen, was the start of a wonderful journey for me!

To my friend, Dawn Dancing Otter, who immortalizes, in my mind, what a strong, heart-centered woman is!

To the woman whom I affectionately call my adopted daughter for beta reading the book - thank you, Alysia.

To my wonderful mother-in-law, who is always willing to be a beta reader - thank you, Mickey.

To my friends, Tim, Chad, and Solandra, for quickly agreeing to be beta readers for this book – thank you.

I would like to acknowledge my wife, Tina, who is always there for me and willing to read whatever I place in front of her, no matter how scattered it may be. Thank you, Tina.

In Love,

L. Neil Thrussell

To the tiny voices in my dreams that won't let me stop writing…

Thank you!

Contents

Misery 1

Ireland 17

Let My Education Begin 23

The Unveiling 31

Contemplation 41

The Apprenticeship 53

Hidden in Plain Sight 59

Digging Deep (er) 67

Into the Chaos of Night 77

A New Day is Dawning 85

So it Begins… In Earnest 183

Divine Timing 197

Into the Unknown 225

New Beginnings 261

Books also by L. Neil Thrussell 267

About the Author 271

Alchemy of the Heart: Shavon Sun Cloud

Misery

This was the very moment in time I had been waiting for all my life. I had spent six gruelling months saving up for this very instant. I could feel my heart racing with excitement. I stayed six months longer at a job I detested, in a town I hated, in an apartment I loathed, with people I couldn't wait to leave behind, so that I could be standing here at this very moment. I breathed in a huge, deep breath. To say that I was miserable before this instant would have been the biggest understatement of the century.

Now, here I was a few minutes away from taking the most significant step in my entire freaking life. I could taste and smell the excitement in the air. Each of the last five days with Master Trainer Mike Realms had been entirely awe-inspiring/completely life-changing/ worth every single sacrifice I had experienced. These past five days and nights had been genuinely magical and had transformed my life completely. This week had been freaking awesome!

I was a changed man. I was a new man. It was like I was about to be born again. I had focus, vision, and a real purpose for my life. I was on fire. I was going to take on the world. I was freaking ready. "Come on, world! I am ready for you!" I joyfully thought to myself as I waited my turn in line.

Alchemy of the Heart: Shavon Sun Cloud

I was awash with positive vibes. I was literally bouncing up and down on the spot, like a child waiting his turn to go to the bathroom. My body was tingling with nervous energy. Three more people to go, and then it would be my turn. Mike Realms always ended his big five-day life purpose events with a fire walk. The moment I discovered this, I knew without a shadow of a doubt, that I needed to do this work. I felt deep within my soul that once I completed the walk, I would be utterly unstoppable. It was my time, and I knew it!

I looked around. Two more people to go. The noise, the chaos, was almost overwhelming. I was so excited and nervous at the same time that I could taste bile in my mouth. The thought, "Damn, this is going to be good!" raced through my head. I was a starving rat at a buffet.

One of the always-smiling fire walk assistants came over and stood before me, bellowing at me, "Ground yourself and stay focused!" I grinned. He bellowed again, "Ground yourself like we showed you." I fought down my excitement as I closed my eyes and began to imagine that my feet were gigantic roots that extended deep into the ground, and from there, I continued to believe that they stretched out for hundreds of feet in all directions. I breathed in and breathed out. My frantic heart rate began to slow down, the tingling sensation in my body began to evaporate, and an overwhelming sense of peace and inner knowing enveloped my whole being. It was like I was now wrapped in a giant marshmallow of love and protection.

I don't know how long I had been grounding for, but it was long enough for the person in front of me to go and complete their walk. Somehow, I managed to hear, "Okay mate, it's your turn. Go!"

At the same time, I felt a tap on my shoulder indicating for me to move forward.

I stepped out onto the sizzling hot coals; it was like I was walking on a warm tile floor and not the near 1000°F hot fiery embers that I was actually walking on. With each new step, I could feel the excitement in my body returning. Here I was, walking on fire. I was amazed. "I am actually doing a fire walk!" My mind began racing. I was actually walking on flipping freaking hot embers! I could taste victory. I only had a mere fifteen feet to go. I was the man; I was on fire. I chuckled at the irony of my thought.

I heard my name, "Devin, over here!" I turned and saw that my new retreat friend, Ali, had his camera out. I turned slightly, waved, and smiled. The pain was instant and intense.

I awoke the next day in the hospital to discover I had second degree burns to twenty-five percent of not one, but both my feet. The doctor told me, "You'll need to stay off your feet for a couple weeks. But other than that, you should have no long-term damage to your feet. You are very fortunate!"

Alchemy of the Heart: Shavon Sun Cloud

The truth was, I didn't feel lucky. I felt like a complete and utter loser. I didn't finish the fire walk. I spent all my savings on a program that I didn't complete. I couldn't even keep my focus on a damn fire walk. How the heck was I going to be able to do anything? I was fifteen feet from the end, and I failed! I failed miserably.

Once again I felt like a total failure. Now I had to go back to a job I hated because, simply put, that's what losers do - they go back to their dead-end jobs, with their dead-end friends and live a miserable existence that wouldn't amount to a hill of beans. In my mind I did everything right and what did God make me do? He had me fail and fail so badly that I made the news as the only loser that didn't make the entire fire walk.

The only good part, if there was a good part out of this whole stupid ordeal, was that I was still on my mother's health insurance, so she didn't have to sell her house for my hospital bill.

Yes, I still lived in the same town I grew up in, I still lived close to my mom, and yes, I even went over every week to see her. Well, what do you expect? It didn't cost me anything to do laundry at her place, and she always fed me. Of course, I went to see her!

The truth was I wasn't even supposed to be under her insurance, but we lied to the insurance company to save me $200.00 a month. We said I was still in school and lived at home.

Alchemy of the Heart: Shavon Sun Cloud

I couldn't even imagine what my mother thought when she got a call, "Hi, this is such-n-such from Mike Realm's Training Academy. Your son, the dimwit, was unable to follow clear and precise instructions, and he burned his feet to a crisp while doing a fire walk. It should be noted that 5,999 other people did the walk safely and he was the only loser that couldn't do it."

My mother would have responded with something like, "Fire walk? He said he was going to a workshop to discover his passion, what he wants to do with his life!" Then she would give off this annoying snort and continue, "He's just like his father. He is such a dreamer. He wouldn't listen to me, and now you say he's burned his feet. He and his father are both idiots!"

Then the hospital would phone up and say, "Your son needs to stay in the hospital for a few days. Oh! And just so you know, your premiums are going to skyrocket to the roof for the rest of your life because of your dim-witted son's little incident fire walking."

She would then caustically respond, "He's just like his father. He's an idiot. He's leaving me with all the bills, again, just like his idiot father!"

After the doctor broke the news to me, I spent pretty much every hour of that first day that I was awake berating myself for my stupidity. The bright and lively green hospital walls decorated with inspirational posters with quotes on love, faith, and belief only made me feel worse. It was like they were purposely rubbing my failure in my face.

The only good part of the day was that I got to spend it all doped up on painkillers. Good painkillers! Serious drugs!

The next morning was not one of my finest moments either. Within ten minutes of the nursing station shift change, my nurse pretty much told me to get out of her sight. "You are behaving like a whiny little baby," she scolded. "Yes, you've burned your feet, but it's not the end of the world. You're behaving like a spoiled rotten child. Take your wheelchair and your sorry arse to the main floor and out into the courtyard for a little bit of fresh air. It will do you good!"

So, with the added insult of being told I was a baby to destroy my already-damaged delicate pride, I hastily exited my room in a huff. I steered myself to the elevator and rode down to the main floor, arriving on the ground level in a terribly foul mood. When the elevator doors opened, I was assailed by a sheer wall of noisy people milling about the elevators, making it extremely difficult for me to get out without getting my burned feet touched in the mayhem.

I tried my best to be polite with, "Could you please move. Excuse me," but my tone was somewhat short and terse. It didn't seem to really matter as I still couldn't get out of the elevator, let alone away from it.

The crowd, the noise, the futility of my situation on top of the nurse calling me a baby just seemed to overwhelm me. A sense of anger, hopelessness, and rage boiled over. I found myself uncharacteristically bellowing, "Get out of my way people!" The volume of my shout took many by surprise. They were now a bunch of deer caught in the headlights of the oncoming traffic, frozen and unable to understand what I just said.

Hastily I took in a breath and was set to yell even louder at the insolent crowd when I heard beside me, "Excuse us, make way." Then I felt my wheelchair suddenly lurch forward. As the wheelchair rocketed forward, I kind of felt like Moses as the wall of people magically parted before me… I mean 'us'! Us, being me and whoever was now pushing my wheelchair.

I heard this beautifully divine feminine voice behind me, "Excuse us, make way, look out." The voice had a magical, spellbinding, strong Irish lilt to it. My saviour was a woman!

The crowds parted, and soon we were out of the horrendous gaggle of people. The voice from behind me asked, "Where you plannin' on endin' up?"

I crisply responded, "The courtyard."

Alchemy of the Heart: Shavon Sun Cloud

I heard her excitedly exclaim, "Grand!" Then her walking tempo promptly picked up.

We zigged and zagged a few times, dodging people and other wheelchairs. In a few short moments, we came to a slow, rolling halt in the quiet solitude of the courtyard.

I felt her reach down and deftly apply the wheelchair brakes. I may have been in a pissy mood a few mere seconds ago but listening to her cheerful lilt had strangely lifted my spirits.

I tried to turn and face my saviour, but before I could do that, she was around to the front of my wheelchair. I finally got my first glance at my long-haired saviour. Gracefully, she pulled a nearby chair over and sat directly in front of me.

I could only helplessly stare. I had never seen a more beautiful woman in my life. She had the most amazing red hair and captivating green eyes. Her complexion was flawless.

She smiled, "I'm glad you find the packagin' so appealing Mr. ___?" She looked at me expectantly, waiting for a response.

I was completely awestruck and unable to answer. I was still deeply and profoundly enthralled with the glimmering colour of her emerald eyes, sparkling in the light of the morning sun. It was like she had somehow captured the entire cosmic beauty of the whole universe within the depths of her green eyes.

Alchemy of the Heart: Shavon Sun Cloud

She tried again, "It wasn't just a few short moments ago that you weren't so lost for words, Mr. ___?"

It seemed like an eternity, but in truth, it was probably only a second or two before I was able to draw the strength to blink. I blushed sheepishly, "Sorry, I come from a small town where beautiful women don't randomly come to my rescue."

She wasn't exactly staring at me, though she was intently looking at me. Somehow, I sensed she was searching for something. It felt like her eyes were boring through me into my soul. It began to make me feel very uncomfortable; I almost started to feel like I was standing naked in front of her. That intent look made me feel like she was seeing me with more than her eyes.

To break my uneasiness I offered, "My name is Devin, Devin Jones."

She grinned, "I don't usually rescue rude people. But for some reason, I was drawn to save you from the angry mob. They looked like they were ready to swarm you and thrash you within an inch of your life, Devin Jones." She playfully continued, "Generally, Devin Jones, I think when one's feet are sprawled forward in a vulnerable position one doesn't anger the crowds unless they're lookin' for a quick and intensive lesson in pain management." She cocked her head to the side and chuckled, "Generally!"

Alchemy of the Heart: Shavon Sun Cloud

I sighed, "Generally, I wouldn't either, but I have been having a bad couple of days..." I looked as intently as I could into her eyes, adding "Ms. ___?" while thinking to myself, "Two can play this look-deep-into-another-person's-eyes routine!"

I was thoroughly unnerved as it appeared she really hadn't taken her eyes off me. It seemed that every time I made eye contact with her, her eyes were already looking deeply into mine. It almost felt like she was a cyborg from some science-fiction show and she was somehow scanning me with her beautiful green eyes.

She broke her silence, "Me name is Shavon, Shavon Sun Cloud."

I reached over with my hand extended, "Pleased to meet you, Shavon."

Shavon leaned forward and gently took my hand, "Wonderful to meet you, Devin."

I expected her to let go of my hand after a second or two - three seconds tops - but she didn't. She looked me in the eyes again and asked, "What's troublin' you, Devin? I see you hurt your feet. What's the story behind the bandaged feet?"

Shavon's heartwarming presence, her simple question and genuine care touched me. Astonishingly, emotions that I didn't even know I had suddenly burst to the surface. I was taken completely and utterly by surprise. All in the same instant I felt angry, sad, ashamed, lost, and riddled with guilt. I was reduced to a five-year-old Devin that threw up all over her.

Like a dormant volcano, I was suddenly spewing lava all over her, and there was nothing I could do to stop the flow. "My mother never loved me. . . My dad left me. . . My sister left the house when she was sixteen. . . I never had any friends. . . Anything I was good at I was never supported in . . . No one ever really liked me. . . I don't know what to do. . . I am massively in debt. . . I hate my job. . . I am not good at anything. . . I did the most incredible program just two days ago. . . I screwed that up too. . ."

During all my verbal vomiting Shavon kept smiling and never once took her eyes off mine, nor did she let go of my hand. She just kept looking into my eyes without any apparent judgment. For the very first time in my life, I felt heard. I felt heard and I didn't once feel judged. It was an incredibly cathartic experience!

Then just as suddenly as it started, the flow of words and emotions stopped. Feeling slightly embarrassed at my verbal diarrhea I looked at Shavon, smiled sheepishly and asked, "So what brings you to the hospital?"

Shavon smiled back, "A friend of a friend knew I was in town and asked if I would deliver a wee package to her friend. "

I inquired, "Was this person a friend of yours? Were they working this morning?"

Alchemy of the Heart: Shavon Sun Cloud

Shavon shook her head, "I've never met her before today."

I stared at Shavon in disbelief at the sheer madness of what she was saying. "So, a friend of a friend asked you to deliver a parcel to someone you don't even know?"

"They did."

I was almost speechless. Almost! I incredulously asked, "And you did this before 7:00 in the morning for a total stranger!?!?"

Shavon was enjoying my confusion and was now grinning from ear to ear, "I don't even live in this city. If you want the whole story, I was in Miami for a workshop last week, and I hung around for a while so I could meet up with her."

My mouth flopped open, "But we are in St. Petersburg!"

Shavon laughed, "Devin! You may have thought you lost everythin' in the last couple of days, but you do still have a great sense of geography."

The look of confusion on my face shifted into a look of total perplexity, "So, where do you live?"

Shavon grinned, "Ireland, in a wee town called Kilmessan, close to Dublin."

In awe and total disbelief, I said, "So you travel all the way from Ireland to Florida to do a workshop…"

Alchemy of the Heart: Shavon Sun Cloud

Shavon interrupted me, "I was here to lead the workshop, Devin."

Dipping my head slightly in recognition of her correction to my story, I said, "You came to Florida to lead a workshop..."

Shavon nodded her head as I sputtered and continued in my astounded state, "Then you make your way to St. Petersburg to give this person that you don't know a gift from a friend of a friend??"

A delightful smile splashed across Shavon's face, "That sums it up nicely."

The perplexity of my facial expressions telegraphed my words even before I spoke, "Why???"

Impishly she laughed, "I want so badly to tease you and say, "because!", but I fear that would add to your overall frustration. Devin, when me friend asked me to deliver the gift, me heart knew there was a reason I was being asked. I didn't know the reason, but I know there is always a reason. So, of course, I said I would."

My mind was overwhelmingly awash from this bizarre concept of staying in a country for almost a week so that you could deliver a package to a friend's friend! I could not help it, but the line from the movie, *The Princess Bride*, kept leaping into my consciousness, "Inconceivable!"

Alchemy of the Heart: Shavon Sun Cloud

Shavon smiled, reached out and gently put her hand on my arm, "When you follow the path of God/Spirit/the Universe/ or whatever higher power you believe in, you eventually learn to trust. Look at today. I don't know for sure but there is a great chance that me trip was divinely orchestrated so we would meet, Devin."

I snorted, "Yeah, right!"

Shavon let go of my arm and sat back in the chair, a look of deep concentration quickly etching across her face. I could feel my ears tingle with the effects of my embarrassment. I stammered, "I didn't mean to hurt your feelings."

Shavon flashed a beautiful, radiant smile, "You didn't hurt my feelin's. I'm gettin' a thought, a feelin', and I'm just sittin' with it." Then she sat quietly.

I was unsure if she was telling the truth. I didn't really have a lot of experience in dealing with women of any age, so, I really didn't know!

Shavon snapped out of her trance-like state and excitedly reached forward and touched my arm again, "You're comin' to Ireland with me, Devin!"

I couldn't help but sputter in pure shocked surprise, "Pardon me!? I don't even know you!"

Alchemy of the Heart: Shavon Sun Cloud

Shavon squealed in absolute delight, "That's so true and that's what makes it an even more perfect adventure for you!" Shavon had a beautiful impish smile that totally disarmed me and put me completely at ease.

"Devin, what do you need to know about me?"

Without waiting for my reply Shavon grabbed the back of my wheelchair, reached over me and released the brakes on my chair and commanded, "Let's go to the coffee shop!"

We were off and soon zipping our way through the morning hospital congestion.

Alchemy of the Heart: Shavon Sun Cloud

Alchemy of the Heart: Shavon Sun Cloud Ireland

Nervously I sat back into my business class seat as the plane was abruptly pushed back from the jetway. I couldn't help but smile like a four-year-old on Christmas morning seeing his Christmas presents for the very first time. I was officially going to Dublin! I almost had to pinch myself. This all seemed too good to be true.

I could scarcely believe the vortex of chaos that my life had been in for the last three weeks. From meeting Shavon to agreeing to almost blindly follow this woman whom I barely knew, to a country I did not know, to do things I did not know about, for reasons I did not fully understand... was a crazy experience. Even wilder yet, I was going on someone else's dime! Shavon was paying for my flight. I could scarcely believe my ears when she said, "Your comin' to Ireland, and I'm goin' to pay for it."

It was surprising enough for me to digest that she was paying for my trip, but she actually paid to fly me to Ireland business class! I have never flown anywhere in business class.

The truth be known, I had only been in one other plane before today's flight - a little Cessna jobby, flying over the Everglades. Needless to say I was a little out of my league and entirely awestruck by the whole flying business class experience.

Alchemy of the Heart: Shavon Sun Cloud

Settling back into my seat, I closed my eyes and reflected upon the weeks leading up to my flight. Shavon stayed with me for most of the first drug-free day while I was in hospital and part of the next day, right up to the moment that I was discharged from the hospital. She even went with me to my mom's place, where I would be staying for the next few weeks while I recovered.

My mother was not overly impressed with me coming home with my feet all bandaged up. She was even less impressed with me 'talking nonsense' about quitting my job, uprooting myself and going to Ireland with a woman that I had just met.

My mother wasn't typically a screamer or a yeller, but for the last three weeks that we spent together, she definitely was. I will give her credit, though, since her last words to me were, "You know I love you and as you can guess, I am really not happy you're doing this. But you will always have a home if this doesn't turn out well."

She gave me a tearful, bone-crushing bear hug and told me, "Be safe!" Then she fled, leaving me standing in line to get through the TSA screening feeling slightly bewildered. Historically my mother was not an overly affectionate person. I could count on a couple hands in recent memory the number of times my mother hugged me! Or I hugged her.

Alchemy of the Heart: Shavon Sun Cloud

Most of my limited circle of friends couldn't understand why I was going either. Once they saw a picture of Shavon, they instantly thought that it was all about lust and I was going to Ireland to get lucky. In one of my earlier stages of life I would've loved it to be that reason, but as pretty and desirable as she was, for some odd quirk I could not explain, I saw her more like a teacher and not an object of my affection. Don't get me wrong. I had feelings for her, but for some weird reason, they weren't sexual.

What I did know about my trip to Ireland was that Shavon had a bunch of workshops and classes she was going to teach, and I was to be some form of sherpa or a jack-of-all-trades for her. I was also going to get the opportunity to attend her trainings for free once all my work was done. What that would look like was entirely unknown to me, and for some odd, inexplicable reason I was ok with that.

The first leg of the trip was Miami to Munich. As the plane levelled off to its final flight elevation I reached over into my backpack and grabbed the book I was to have read by the time I got to Dublin. I smirked. The only stipulation Shavon put on my trip to Dublin was that I was to have read Carlos Castaneda's book *"The Teachings of Don Juan: A Yaqui Way of Knowledge."* I was also instructed to regard it as a story, a work of fiction, but I was to remain open to the fact that parts of the fiction experiences could indeed be true. In Shavon's own words, "Devin, the truth is far stranger than fiction."

Whether the book was fiction or not, it had me curious and scared at the same time. Was Shavon going to be feeding me drugs and traipsing me about in darkened rooms in some kind of crazy drug-induced ceremonies? Was she part of some ancient, mystic cult? I was scared, but definitely curious!

When I landed at the Dublin airport, I was immediately accosted… not by smell or sights, but by the language. I definitely knew I was not in America anymore. I assumed Irish people spoke English like I did, or even like the British people on the television did. Shavon had a beautiful, gentle lilt to her spoken word, but what the general population spoke here was entirely foreign to me. I strongly suspected it was alien to the very planet, as well!

It took me forever to decipher what the gruff customs agent asked me. "Ow lahng ye plannin' to stay in Oireland?" and "Is yahr stay 'ere business or pleasure?"

I thought I got on and off the wrong freaking plane. My mind was awash with, "Where the hell is this place he called Oireland"? I stammered, "Pardon me?"

The stern agent looked at me like I was utterly deaf or stunned, and quite possibly both. He spoke again, this time drawing out the whole sentence as if I was intellectually challenged -which I might

Alchemy of the Heart: Shavon Sun Cloud

be by Ireland's standards. "Ow - lahng - ye – plannin' - to - stay - in – Oireland?"

Then like a car that hasn't been run in a while, my brain finally warmed up to the agent's distinct dialect. I sputtered, "Oireland... You mean Ireland?"

He grinned, "Oi mean 'Oireland.' Oi'm guessin' ye 'aven't been taught to speak loike a proper Oirishman, yet?"

I finally was able to catch on to what he was telling me, so I replied with a smirk on my face, "First time out of the United States. I have had not had the opportunity to learn a civilized tongue!"

The agent smiled, stamped my passport, and sent me on my way with, "Av a great visit."

With that, I was on my way. I collected my suitcase and excitedly headed towards the reception area where I was to meet Shavon.

Alchemy of the Heart: Shavon Sun Cloud

Alchemy of the Heart: Shavon Sun Cloud

Let My Education Begin

The sensor on the frosted glass doors separating me from the reception area tracked my approaching movement and the doors opened with a whoosh. Fifteen yards ahead of me was Shavon. She looked absolutely incredible. The sun backlit her beautiful red hair, and she had a halo around her head like the halos all the saints have on the stained-glass images in the giant old cathedrals.

I couldn't help but smile inwardly. I thought I was excited to be in 'Oireland' but Shavon looked even more excited. She was bouncing and enthusiastically waving to me like a teenager at her first rock concert. She called out, "Devin. Devin. Over 'ere lad."

I slowly weaved my way through the milling crowd. It appears airport etiquette in Ireland is to do all your heartfelt greetings right in the middle of the walkway and within five feet of the doorway! I only had to walk fifteen yards to reach Shavon, but because of the congestion, it felt like I had traversed an entire continent and it took two full years!

Finally, I made it to within a yard of Shavon. She gleefully swooped in and threw her arms around me, embracing me with a big ole' welcoming hug. "Welcome to Oireland, Devin."

I hugged her and excitedly squealed back, "Thank you, and thank you for inviting me."

Alchemy of the Heart: Shavon Sun Cloud

Shavon grinned, "Don't be thankin' me yet. Ye've lots of work to do." She let go of her embrace, "Starval? Knackered?"

I laughed, "Your accent is a little thicker now that you are home."

Shavon chuckled, "Oi'm not the one with the accent. Ye've the accent." She turned and headed towards a door, "This way."

I wasn't nervous to be travelling to Ireland on my own until that moment. The realization slowly seeped into my tired head that I truly was a foreigner in a foreign land. I was the one that spoke funny. I was the one with the strange perceptions and attitudes. Everyone else was going about their business as if all things were normal. Their speech, mannerisms, and customs were normal to them. I was the one that was going to have to adapt! Truly a foreign concept to me.

She hurriedly stepped through the door and immediately headed off toward what appeared to be the parking lot.

My lessons in adaptation came fast and furious. My first lesson in adaption to the Irish culture was sitting on the wrong side of the car as a passenger. My second lesson came immediately after that, as I experienced the terror of hurtling down freeways in a vehicle that was smaller than my ATV at home, on the wrong freaking side of the road.

Shavon miraculously, as if she received a gift from the gods, sensed my nervousness. Maybe it was the fact that I had both hands stretched out in front of me glued to the dashboard in the universal crash position that gave it away. Or the fact that I hadn't spoken a word once we burst onto the freeway with thousands of cars speeding everywhere!

Or maybe she noticed that my face had lost all its color and I looked like some pasty-faced zombie. Whatever was her clue, she asked, "Nervous?"

Any sense of masculine pride I may have had in my body left me the moment the front tire touched the freeway. "Nervous? No! Not really. I think the words I am looking for are terrified, petrified, scared to death!"

Shavon was mortified, "Me drivin' is not that brutal!"

Nervously I replied, "Your driving skills are excellent. It's just that you are driving on the wrong side of the road, Shavon. It is taking all the strength I can muster in my body to not reach over and grab the steering wheel and reef on it to get us back onto the right side of the road!"

Shavon snorted, "Oi know. Oi 'ad the same feelin' the first time Oi went to America!"

I meekly squeaked out, "If one was to fess up, this is the first time I have ever been out of the country. "

Alchemy of the Heart: Shavon Sun Cloud

Shavon interrupted me with a deep, insincere mocking tone in her voice, "Really, Oi would 'av never noticed!"

I let Shavon's comment slide by and continued, with hopes of salvaging any pride I had left, "The truth is I have never left Florida before, either. I saw no purpose in galivanting around the countryside. I couldn't see that there was a purpose to it!"

The pitch of Shavon's voice instantly raised to one of total flabbergast and disbelief, "What do ye mean ye couldn't see value in travel? Travel is the greatest education a person could ever receive. It opens up yahr stagnant personal views of the world to the fact that there is more than one religion, and more than one particular type of grub. Ye learn that no matter what faith ye 'ave, or what country ye travel to, a mother's or father's love is universal."

Just as suddenly as Shavon exploded all over me, she was now absolutely calm. Gracefully, like nothing had occurred just two seconds before, she turned and glanced towards me as she continued rocketing in and out of traffic in the aluminum soda can she called her car, "Sorry, Devin, as ye can tell Oi'm passionate about me belief in travel as an educational tool."

With my hands still glued to the front of the dash - petrified I was going to die in a fiery head-on collision – I managed, "Really? I never noticed!"

Alchemy of the Heart: Shavon Sun Cloud

Shavon gleefully laughed, "Yahr not an epic liar! Whatever ye do, don't start!"

A minute later she added, "We're goin' to meet a few of me lasses for a bite of grub just up the way."

Shavon quickly shifted my terror-filled ride down the freeway by quickly pulling off the main road onto a new sort of living hell... A single lane divided highway with no lane markings on it!

I thought for sure this was it. We were going to die in some head-on collision. I was going to die within my first couple hours of being in a foreign country! This was going to be my penance for leaving the good ole' U.S.A. My mind raced, "My mother is probably still mad at me, so she won't even accept my body if they ship it back home. I will probably be buried in some unmarked grave in Ireland. Or, if they put a headstone on my grave, the tombstone will say something like, 'Even his mother didn't want him!'"

I did my best to keep my attention on the scenery. I couldn't help but notice with my terror-heightened senses, "Ireland is a very beautiful country!"

Shavon smiled, "Tank ye!" Her smile was filled with immense pride. I was keenly aware that she loved her country as much as I loved mine!

Alchemy of the Heart: Shavon Sun Cloud

As we sped along the laneway, I finally noticed there were hedges all along the road. Everything was so green. There were many ancient, stone buildings and a sign to a castle. What really shocked me was the number of golf courses that I saw in the short time we had been driving.

"The castle back there. Is it a castle with a moat and draw bridge?" I asked with a little hint of hope and excitement.

Shavon dashed my enthusiasm with a shake of her head, "Just a really big, fancy house."

We drove on in silence for a few moments, then Shavon glanced over at me, a big warm smile painted over her entire face, "Ye can relax soon – we're almost there."

"Where is there?" I asked.

She replied, "Kilmessan, and grub!" There was a sense of calm and happiness in her voice.

A few minutes later we pulled into the mighty - town? village? - of Kilmessan. A quick left, then a right, another right, and we pulled up across from a pub.

I questioned, "A pub?"

Shavon gleefully laughed as she confirmed, "A pub's always a master place to eat in Oireland."

Alchemy of the Heart: Shavon Sun Cloud

With Shavon's words of wisdom, we got out and entered my third lesson of adaptation to a new culture - heading into a pub mid-day. The few times in my life I have frequented a bar it was never until after 9:00 or 10:00 pm. It was also never for the sole purpose of eating food!

Lessons four, five and six came at me like a tsunami. We walked into the pub, and it was like a small horde of people descended on us. Okay! Maybe not 'us' per say but Shavon, for sure. The swarm was similar to locusts swarming a grain field. It was biblical in proportion. Apparently, she was a minor celebrity.

Almost at once I was accosted with a constant barrage of slang, "Gas, hatchet, drobes, flyin' it." I had to continually ask for an explanation.

I quickly learned to never ask where a person was from because all the names of the local towns and villages became incomprehensible to my untrained ears. The names all sounded like a bunch of consonants randomly thrown together.

I also learned that pub food was indeed excellent. Shavon ordered food and a beverage for both of us. We had some form of pizza and beer. The beer was a bit thick and dark for my amateur taste, but it did go well with the pizza, even if the pizza appeared to be lacking meat of any kind.

Alchemy of the Heart: Shavon Sun Cloud

An astute man would have known that no meat on a pizza was some form of foreshadowing, but I was apparently not so astute. It took me a few days before I realized that mealtime with Shavon was going to be strictly vegetarian.

Alchemy of the Heart: Shavon Sun Cloud

The Unveiling

I arrived in 'Oireland' on a Wednesday. We headed to Shavon's small farm (acreage) where I had a little time to get used to the language, the food, and her driving about the countryside without me going into full-scale panic attacks again. By Friday we were up, packed, and off to a retreat center (that I could not pronounce even if I tried!) before first light.

My jobs during the workshop were many. I was at the registration desk. I also ensured Shavon ate. I herded people back into the workshop and ceremonies, as necessary. I took money from participants for workshops, seminars, and book sales. It was a pleasant surprise to discover Shavon had written two books on 'Celtic Shamanism' and one on plant medicine.

Above all during the entire weekend, no matter where I was or what was going on, I listened. I got to be very good at doing a myriad of things and still being able to listen to her teachings. Truth be known, I found the lessons fascinating.

It was late Sunday evening when the door clicked shut behind the last straggler of the weekend workshop. Apparently, there are always a few participants reluctant to leave the magic of a workshop. They probably dread facing the world again after a truly magical experience.

Alchemy of the Heart: Shavon Sun Cloud

I stopped packing up and turned to Shavon. She opened her mouth to speak, but I ran roughshod over her, "You were hatchet. It was jammers, and my mind is in tatters!" *(Translation: Absolutely brilliant, packed full of information, and my mind is completely destroyed.)*

She squealed with delight, "That was awesome, Devin. Ye've got it!"

Apparently, my American to Irish and my Irish to American translator was now working seamlessly, "Thank you!"

Before Shavon could add to her thoughts I asked, "Where the heck did you learn all that stuff you taught all weekend? It was absolutely brilliant. I loved it."

Shavon waited, looking like she was waiting for me to ask more.

I smiled, "I am done."

Shavon spoke, "Let's finish packin' up and go eat. Then Oi'll answer yahr question, Devin. Deal?"

I was already ravenously hungry, so it was an easy choice to make, "Deal!"

We packed up the unsold books and unused workshop materials in silence for about twenty minutes before we found ourselves looking around for more tasks to do. I broke the silence, "I think we are done."

Alchemy of the Heart: Shavon Sun Cloud

Shavon nodded her head, "Yahr correct."

Shavon had previously arranged for us to stay one additional night at the retreat center, so we didn't need to leave until the morning. I couldn't believe I was about to say this, because in Florida I drove everywhere, but I really needed to get out and stretch my legs. With a tiny hint of questioning in my voice I spoke, "When we were driving here, I saw a pub about five hundred yards back the ways. Want to go get a bite to eat there?"

Shavon nodded, "Please. Oi need the walk."

"Okay let's get our coats and meet in the front lobby in a couple minutes," was my response.

Shavon started heading toward her room, "See ye in a couple minutes!"

The temperature was a little chilly, but it felt good to stretch the legs.

Shavon started the conversation with, "Me mother told me stories of old Oirish folklore as a child, and Oi was always interested. Me mother was a masterful storyteller. She could make the story of cleanin' toilets a magical experience."

I asked, "Is she still alive?"

Shavon lowered her head, a sudden sadness overtaking her, "She's gone to the other side. She came down with breast cancer two years ago, and they caught it too late. She lived for three months after the initial diagnosis. But, in a strange, crazy way, it was a delightful time for us both!"

Our conversation halted as we arrived at the pub. As soon as we entered, I was struck by the friendly, jocular atmosphere in the pub. No surprise to me it was full. I highly suspected it was full of regular patrons.

The hostess found us a table. It wasn't going to be a quiet, off-to-the-side table, or way in the back by North American standards, but for Irish pub standards, we were away from the general noise as much as we were going to get!

We both ordered a Guinness and the late-night supper special.

Once our beers arrived Shavon started talking again, "Me mother began tellin' me stories again. This time it was tales Oi never knew she knew. Tales me teachers told me. It was then Oi discovered that me mother was a druid. She knew the many teachings that took me years to learn."

I looked perplexed at Shavon, "Why didn't she tell you she was a druid or, at least, a shaman?"

Shavon smiled, "Oi asked her that. Ye know what she told me?"

It was my turn to smile, "Uh, No?"

Alchemy of the Heart: Shavon Sun Cloud

With a hint of seriousness she continued, "Me mother was taught by an old schoolteacher, and she believed ye 'ave to be born into a shaman family and raised by a shaman and carry on the traditions of a shaman to be called a shaman. Me mother's parents were not shamans, so she felt she couldn't call herself a shaman."

I interjected, "Does that make you one?"

Shavon smiled, "Devin, yahr gettin' ahead of the story! Patience."

Mockingly, I dropped my head in shame, "Sorry!"

Shavon laughed and continued, "Devin, this will add some context to why Oi responded so passionately to yahr comment about travel."

I was somewhat confused at the mention of travel and Shavon's mother, but I didn't interrupt. I let her continue.

"Me mother knew that if she taught me her secrets Oi would not go and see the world, and she would 'ave none of that. As a young woman me mother wanted to travel and see the world… But times were different for women back when me mother was younger. In the '80s women were just startin' to explore the world on their own. It would 'ave been unheard of for an Oirish woman on a shamanic path to see the world.

To complicate things, she got pregnant and married me father at a very young age. Don't get me wrong. Me father loved me mother, and they loved each other fiercely. Me father encouraged her to pursue her shamanic dreams…. just not in other countries!

Me father farmed the land Oi currently live on. This gave me mother and me strong ties to this land, this area, and our Celtic heritage."

Quietly, I interrupted Shavon, "Your father is dead? I mean he is on the other side?"

Shavon took my interruption in stride, nodding, "He is on the other side. He died of cirrhosis of the liver. His love of the drink took him when Oi was fifteen."

I offered a heartfelt, "I am sorry."

Shavon looked up and into my eyes, "Me too!"

I searched for words and tenderly interjected, "You said your father loved your mother… But you didn't say he loved you. Did he love you?"

A small tear rolled down Shavon's face, "Without question." She paused and then added, "He was considered a good farmer by many, but he was an even better singer. He wrote epic ballads for me. He would entertain the pub for hours with his singin'. His songs were always about his three loves - beer, me mother, and me!"

Alchemy of the Heart: Shavon Sun Cloud

Our meal arrived. It looked awesome. Salad, roasted potatoes, gravy, and a whole whack of carrots. It tasted just as impressive as it looked.

Shavon continued in between mouthfuls, "Me mother wanted me to travel, and travel is what Oi did. What she forgot to instill in me was the desire to come 'ome more often. Oi came back infrequently and not for long periods.

When me mother discovered she had cancer she didn't want treatment of any kind. She just wanted to travel. We went to Peru, Ecuador, Mexico, Spain and Egypt. We visited and talked non-stop for nine glorious weeks. We were in Egypt when we knew it was time to come 'ome. We came back 'ere, and three weeks later she passed!"

I reached out and tenderly put my hand on top of hers, "I am sorry!"

A tear rolled down Shavon's right cheek, "Me too… Those nine weeks together were absolutely magical. Oi learned more about Shamanism in those nine weeks than Oi learned in me previous ten years of study under all me masters. Me mother was an incredible woman and a masterful teacher."

Shavon's energy shifted to a place of happiness. I took my hand off hers.

Alchemy of the Heart: Shavon Sun Cloud

She continued with her story, "Ye asked where Oi learned what Oi taught this weekend. The story is complicated because Oi was taught by many masters... Even one whose path Oi 'ave been dedicated to following for more than five years. But the truth is, me mother's lessons in those nine weeks really took me to a new depth in my training. Experiencin' ceremony in the various countries with me mother was truly remarkable. She taught me through stories. It was me mother's gift of tellin' stories that made me able to teach and reach people. Her greatest gift was givin' me her stories. In those last week's together we worked on me tellin' her stories.

When Oi tell a story and the person listenin' figures out the meanin' or lessons behind the story, that's when Oi know Oi'm a teacher worthy of hearin'."

I grinned like the comic book character who had been just hit over the head with a shovel, "Like you telling me in Florida that travelling is a worthwhile endeavour."

Shavon nodded yes and I looked directly into her eyes, my heart softening slightly. Reaching out across the table I took Shavon's hands in mine, "Thank you, Shavon Sun Cloud, for this incredible gift."

Shavon returned the gaze, "Yahr welcome."

Alchemy of the Heart: Shavon Sun Cloud

The hostess broke up our tender moment just a little earlier than I would have liked as she came to clear away our dishes.

Once the hostess left with our dishes I asked, "So, what was your father's gift to you?"

Shavon replied, "Those stories are for another day, Devin. It's time for sleep!"

With that, I got up and paid the bill. Shavon commented, "Ye didn't 'ave to do that. Tank ye!"

I nodded my head in acknowledgment, "You are welcome. I just felt like it."

We left the pub and headed back to the retreat where we called it a night.

Alchemy of the Heart: Shavon Sun Cloud

Alchemy of the Heart: Shavon Sun Cloud

Contemplation

For two early risers, we were up late the next morning. After a leisurely breakfast of coffee, fruit, and a bagel we headed home.

Once we were home, we spent a significant part of the day processing credit cards, completing her paper processes for the returning students, and the new batch of students for the retreat she was doing on the upcoming Friday. We transcribed Shavon's antiquated paper processes into various electronic formats.

This was okay with me since it was a cloudy, rainy morning. In my books, it was definitely okay to stay out of the damp, cold rain.

By late afternoon the sun finally broke through the clouds and was out in full force. This prompted Shavon to declare, "It's time for a walk."

In Florida I would have gone and put on my rubber boots to keep my feet dry, but in Oireland you put on your daisy roots. Either way, we were off exploring the farm.

We had barely left the comfort of the house before Shavon fired off her first question, "Devin, what 'ave ye learned so far?"

I was a little taken aback by the directness of her question, but it was an easy reply for me, "You teach in allegories. There always seem to be messages within messages and it is for the student to figure out the lessons."

Shavon gleeful responded, "Very good, Devin. What else?"

I slyly grinned, knowing full well this is not what she was asking, but this was how I was going to respond, "Your business model is a mess. You are handling pieces of paper three and four times. Each time you handle the paper you have a chance of inducing error and then carrying that error forward."

Shavon snorted, "Good point! But that's not what Oi was askin'."

I smiled that knowing smile you get when you think you got one on your teacher, "I know, but it is what you desperately need to help your business out!"

I shifted my attention back to her question, "Outside of that, I am learning that a person needs to create time for rituals and ceremony. I am discovering rituals are essential to spirituality because the repetition of enacting each ritual provides a focal point for me from the distraction around me, providing me a certain level of comfort and familiarity. Ritual also provides an opportunity to show reverence for being in the moment, moment to moment. I also suspect one of the reasons why church, music, and prayer can be such an uplifting experience is because the weekly rituals reinforce a sense of community.

Alchemy of the Heart: Shavon Sun Cloud

After spending time with you, I am almost certain that the need for ceremony is embedded deep within our DNA. As I reflect upon it now, I am amazed that when a group of people in almost any part of the world get together, we try to do something ceremonially, even if it is just a champagne toast or an announcement of an engagement that calls for three cheers, and the likes of that. I only know the world travelling part based on television shows and not first-hand experience, but I strongly suspect it is true!"

Shavon stopped and gently touched my arm, "Devin, the depth of yahr words is truly astoundin'! Yahr words project deep inner wisdom."

I could feel the blood warm my ears as I began to blush. "Thank you!" was my only response.

Shavon looked at me, "Why're ye blushin'?"

I could feel the tears begin to well up, "You forgot our first meeting?"

Shavon responded softly, "Devin Jones, Oi 'aven't forgotten."

My ears were still red. Tears were ready to burst from my eyes. I took a big breath in and shakily spoke, "I don't doubt the fact that my mother loves me in her own peculiar way, but as a child, I never got words of encouragement. I never heard, "Great job, Devin. We are proud of you."

Instead, I got a lot of, "You are an idiot. You are just like your loser of a father."

My hands began to tremble, "My mother took me to the airport. For the entire drive to the airport, she told me I was silly or stupid for going." I let out a big body wracking sob, "She said I was a fool for trusting you."

Shavon stepped into me and wrapped her arms around me in a body enveloping hug and gently asked, "Why did ye come, Devin Jones?"

I sobbed, "I don't know. What I did know is that you were the first person to ever treat me with such kindness and with no expectations of me. You wanted nothing in return. You just exuded love and compassion. Something that I deeply needed… using your own languaging, Shavon, my soul was aching to be loved! I needed it on a cellular level."

Shavon didn't say another word. She held me for a long time.

Eventually, the feelings of unworthiness subsided from my body. Once the sensation had left, I slowly untangled myself from Shavon's caring embrace. Immediately I faced the mortifying awareness that I had snot running down my face!

What started out as a slow, casual search quickly escalated into a frantic search of my pockets for a tissue, any tissue. In my distressed mind, even a piece of paper would work. I was getting

Alchemy of the Heart: Shavon Sun Cloud

desperate and was just about to use my sleeve when Shavon handed me a tissue.

"Thank you!"

She smiled and responded, "As a go forward, don't go anywhere without a tissue - either for yahrself or another - when Oi'm around."

I blushed slightly and smiled, "Got it."

We both turned in unison and continued our walk. Shavon shared, "Each of us starts down the path of personal betterment, or spiritual quest, for our own reasons. But generally, it's because we 'ave an 'ole deep within us. An 'ole that can be boiled down to a sense of absence, wantin', or longin'.

Oi say this without judgment, Devin. Yahr path, or reason, is the need for love. Ye've a belief that love is missin' from yahr life."

I stammered, "I am embarrassed when you say it like that. It can't be that simple… Can it?"

Shavon chuckled, "Why can't it be that simple, Devin? It's only humankind that makes things so complicated."

I sheepishly responded, "It just seems so… so shallow to say that I am a love-starved man, and I am leading my life looking for love!"

Alchemy of the Heart: Shavon Sun Cloud

Shavon stopped, turned, and touched my arm again, "The truth, Devin, is almost always that pure. Most of the time people's deepest hurt - when distilled to its purest essence - can be perceived by others as that shallow. Yet, when we learn to accept that we can be shallow, and we learn to recognize who we are in all of our imperfections, that's when we truly rise to be the persons we're destined to become.

Devin, Oi fled Oireland. Not because me mother didn't love me, but because Oi couldn't stand our 'ouse without being me daddy's center of attention. He wrote a new song about me almost every two weeks since Oi was a wee lass.

Oi couldn't bear to not be the center of someone's universe. Oi was in search of being the center of someone's - or something's - universe.

Devin, one of humankind's most significant needs is to be loved! We'll tolerate all sorts of abuse just to be loved. Even if it 'arms us mentally or physically, we need and want to be loved!"

Hearing Shavon's story, my heart was breaking. I could only muster up a meek, "I didn't know!"

She let go of my arm and turned and continued our walk. It appeared she was heading to the barn.

"That is the truth, Devin. Ye don't know what Oi've been through to get to where Oi'm now. Same as the day Oi met you. Oi did not know yahr story that put ye into hospital and the story behind yahr anger that day. Oi just saw a soul that was in desperate need of help.

In the most simplistic characterization or diagnosis Oi can offer, Oi left Oireland lookin' for love to fill a void. Devin, ye attended a workshop lookin' for love to fill a void. Yahr feelin' the lack of self-love and the lack of love of a parent.

We're both lookin' to have that void filled. This is not intended to diminish our feelin's or add shame to our beliefs. It's just a simple way to characterize a way of being.

A physician can diagnose ye have a cold or a flu, and the diagnosis doesn't diminish the sensation of a runny nose, sore throat and high fever to yahr body.

When we remove the emotional connection to our actions or way of being, it becomes easier for us to make changes without as many judgements towards ourselves. As an example, Oi recognize that Oi, Shavon Sun Cloud, have a strong sense of needin' to be the center of attention. Recognizin' this need, Oi seek out opportunities for me to be the center of attention. Hence, Oi sing in the pub occasionally."

I stopped, turned, and placed my hand on Shavon's arm, "Thank you for sharing your story with me. I have to admit, I am struggling with how shallow one of my base needs appears to be but – a giant but! - at some level it makes sense. Yet, I think my sense of self-worth wants it to be more complicated than that. I am struggling with this overly simple view of myself."

Shavon smiled, "Ye've done remarkably well to grasp all of this in such a short time. Don't be beatin' yahrself up."

I let go of Shavon's arm, turned, faced the house and snorted, "If our goal is to walk one mile, at this pace it will take us hours. We've barely made it 100 yards from the house."

Shavon giggled, "Always a goal or task with you."

I frowned, "Is that bad?"

Shavon smiled, a deep compassionate smile, "Just an observation, that's all."

Mockingly pouting, I turned and started walking, "Well, then let's continue on and go see the barn."

The barn was of interest to me. I wanted to see what it was made of and learn the history of the barn itself.

I was disappointed, as a city person, to not see any actual animals in the barn... besides pigeons and the signs of a few rats. After we toured the barn, Shavon simply said, "Oi'm famished. Let's go eat."

I eagerly agreed, "Can we try somewhere new?"

Alchemy of the Heart: Shavon Sun Cloud

Shavon teased, "Oh, Oi thought ye'd be tired of pub food. Oi thought we'd go to McDonald's."

I think Shavon chuckled from the shades of gagging green I turned before I was able to speak, "I haven't eaten fast food in many years. I would really prefer not to start now!"

Shavon paused and looked at me like she was appraising me – the way you would appraise a house looking for its faults – and asked, "Really? Ye don't eat fast food?"

Indignation spewed from my mouth, "Yes, it is true. Not every single American male lives on burgers and fries. Yes, I do like soda occasionally. My beer isn't as strong or as thick as your Irish beer. I do like a good ale and a fine glass of wine. I like real food, food that is prepared when you order it, not premade in some factory. I like to enjoy my food, and I appreciate it when it is well made."

Shavon pretended to grab the ends of an invisible dress and curtsied before me, "Sorry me lord, Oi 'ad ye confused for some barbarian from the Americas and not a real cultured lord. Please forgive me."

Adding to the whole imaginary drama I held out my arm, "All is forgiven, my lady." She slid her arm comfortably into mine. We walked arm and arm back to the house, laughing at our silliness for most of the way back.

Alchemy of the Heart: Shavon Sun Cloud

Shavon took me to another village that had a name that I couldn't pronounce - not even when I looked at the English spelling of the name! Oh, my goodness the food at the pub was divine. It was all fresh. Each plate was only prepared as it was ordered. With that being said, dinner was not a speedy event, which gave us more time to converse, and converse is what we did.

We talked about mundane business things - streamlining her business practices, talking with her web designer, her accountant. The conversation took a serious tone when I asked, "I have a question on rituals."

Shavon stopped mid-drink and lowered her wine glass from her lips, "What would ye like to know?"

I was searching for the right words, almost mumbling, as I was unsure where I was going with my line of questioning, "Well, you said ritual and ceremonies were important during our walk today, and at the workshop last weekend, you said pretty much the same thing."

Shavon grinned a knowing smile.

I continued, "So, why aren't we doing rituals or ceremony? I have been here close to a week, and outside of the rituals we did at the workshop, it doesn't appear that we have done any."

Shavon raised her wine glass to her lips and took a small sip. Once she finished her sip, she lowered her drink and looked intently into

Alchemy of the Heart: Shavon Sun Cloud

my eyes with that piercing look she has, like she was seeing deep into me. She was looking past my face and into my very soul!

After what seemed like an eternity - but I highly suspected was only a few seconds - Shavon spoke, "Devin, 'ave ye 'eard the phrase, 'When the student is ready, the teacher will appear?'"

I grinned, "Yes, Mike Realms used it a few times in his program."

Shavon leaned back into her chair, still looking intently into my eyes. "Yahr question is a good one. First off, ye know Oi teach in allegories. Why do ye think Oi would hold off on teachin' ye rituals?"

It was now my time to lean back into my chair. I held her gaze. This was taking on a chess game-like atmosphere. "I can only guess, since I am not you. But that being said, you were waiting to know more about me, to see how I would respond to the change in my environment and see what my interests were."

Shavon smiled and slowly let the intensity of her gaze subside. "Devin, yahr a remarkable man. Yahr ability to grasp situations quickly takes me by surprise. Oi was a far less astute student than ye appear to be. It took me almost two months of being with me teacher before Oi asked her that question."

I grinned a sheepishly wicked grin, "What can I say? I am just that good."

Shavon smiled, "Apparently so."

With impeccable timing, our main course was brought before us.

Alchemy of the Heart: Shavon Sun Cloud

The Apprenticeship

The next morning started early with a light rap on my door. "Let's go," Shavon greeted me through the door. "Dress warmly. We're goin' outside."

I took a peek out the window. It was still dark out. It was not raining, but it had rained that night. I was going to need boots.

I walked to the back landing. As I entered the room, Shavon looked up and flashed me an impish smile, "Good. Yahr dressed warmly... but ye don't need yahr shoes and socks.

"Pardon?" was my stunned response.

Shavon giggled, "No questions asked, Devin, as no answers will be given. Roll up yahr pants a little and take off yahr socks. Let's go outside."

I still had a stunned looked of incredulousness plastered across my face as I stammered, "Really?!?"

Shavon smiled and pointed down to her bare feet. I couldn't help but notice it appeared that her toes were recently polished.... a slightly glossy rosy colour.

I sighed that kind of sigh you give when you don't understand what the heck is going on and you know it is going to happen no matter how much you complain or delay. Reluctantly, I bent down and took off my socks. I stuffed them neatly into my shoes.

Shavon gently commanded, "Okay, let's go." With that, she opened the back door and walked outside. It took me a few deep breaths before I followed Shavon. It is one thing to walk on a warm sandy beach, but walking in the wet, muddy grass is quite another matter.

The first few steps across the grass were enough to confirm my suspicion. Yup! It was cold and wet. Not a pleasant experience for this Florida boy.

Like the disgruntled student I was, I slunk over to where Shavon was standing and grudgingly stood before her.

"Cold and wet, huh?" she asked cheerfully.

My measured response was simply, "Yes!"

"Excellent!"

Her happiness was beginning to wear thin on me. My feet were cold and wet and now, like some sadistic sign from the heavens, it started to rain. Not just a few drops but a nice little downpour. My already gloomy attitude was definitely taking a turn for the worse.

Shavon squealed like a child being told that they could have ice cream on a hot day, "This is awesome!"

Alchemy of the Heart: Shavon Sun Cloud

She excitedly turned to me, "Okay, Mr. Grumpy pants. Oi need ye to do two things and two things only. When ye 'ave a thought, Oi want ye to come back to those two things. Don't scold or chastise yahrself for allowin' other thoughts to enter yahr mind. Just come back to the two things I want ye to focus on. Got it?"

I tried to respond cheerfully, but I suspect it sounded somewhat forced, "Sure!"

Shavon responded, "Excellent! Oi'm going to blindfold ye, and Oi want ye to focus on smilin' and the sensations of yahr feet. Not from a place of judging these sensations, but rather as observations, as if ye were tellin' a third person what these sensations were. As an example, cold, wet, squishy, slimy. Then feel into the sensations. Really feel the cold, the wet and the squishiness."

I was a little dumbfounded, "That's my exercise?"

Shavon didn't think my question called for an answer. She just gently placed a blindfold across my eyes.

I have to admit, it was a freaking good blindfold. I couldn't see a darn thing. Not that I was an expert or anything - I hadn't been blindfolded many times before in my life - but in my mind it was a great blindfold!

Once the blindfold was in place, I sensed Shavon step back and heard her say, "Smile and really feel the sensations."

Alchemy of the Heart: Shavon Sun Cloud

With a heavy sigh, I resigned myself to the fact I was going to be standing in the rain till Shavon thought the exercise was complete. I took a deep breath in and then forced a fake smile on my face. I began to feel the sensations of the wetness on the bottom of my feet and the squishiness between my toes.

Slowly, a real smile crept across my face. The mud and the grass at times felt ticklish on my feet. My big toes and little toes were less sensitive to the sensations of cold than my middle toes. Eventually, the rain disappeared, and I completely immersed myself in the feeling of the ground beneath my feet.

Shavon spoke, "Move around slowly. Experience different pieces of the earth."

I walked through ankle-deep mud and puddles, thick grass, short grass, sand, gravel. I was so immersed in the actual feeling and appreciation of the sensations of my feet that I didn't hear Shavon coming. But I smelled her. She was carrying a cup of coffee. I couldn't help but say, "Your perfume is divine! Ode de coffee."

Shavon giggled, "That's awesome. Put yahr hands out."

I held my hands out and Shavon gently placed the hot cup of coffee in my right hand. Instinctively, my left hand grasped the cup. Now it was nestled between both of my hands like a sacred object. The warmth from the cup seemed to warm my entire body. It was bizarre. Any cold I had been feeling was now gone.

Alchemy of the Heart: Shavon Sun Cloud

Shavon gently commanded, "Drink."

I raised the cup of warmth to my mouth. As I did, I inhaled its deep, rich aroma. It truly was heavenly. Ever so cautiously I took a sip. It wasn't as hot as I thought or expected. I took a much larger sip. My taste buds exploded in rapture. It was pure taste bud heaven. I had never had so many individual experiences from a simple cup of coffee. I got a bold, brash taste at the beginning of my sip, immediately followed by a deep sense of richness, and finally a touch of bitterness as the coffee slid past my tongue and down my throat. It was like tasting coffee for the very first time! It was divine ecstasy. Yet, it was familiar. It was like I always knew the tastes, but I had forgotten, or pushed them aside!

Shavon broke my rapture with, "Lower yahr hands. Oi'm goin' to untie yahr blindfold." I heard her shuffle behind me.

As the blindfold fell away, I was a little blinded by the slight illumination. The sun was just starting to rise on the distant horizon. The pre-dawn light seemed bright to me, like I was experiencing sight with new eyes.

We stood together in silence and watched God paint the day before us. The sunrise was breathtakingly amazing.

After the sun had risen a fair way up into the sky, Shavon turned to me, "How was this experience?"

Alchemy of the Heart: Shavon Sun Cloud

I opened my mouth to speak, then promptly closed it. I was at a loss for words.

Shavon smiled, "Yahr goin' through option two of the two most common responses Oi've encountered with this exercise. Response one is a diatribe of the sheer beauty of the whole experience. Response two is a complete loss of words."

I shrugged my shoulders and grinned, "At least I am normal!"

Shavon laughed, "It appears so." She turned and said, "Let's go eat."

A flicker of disappointment flashed across my face, "I thought we were going to work on ceremony and ritual today?"

Shavon stopped, turned, and faced me. With the slightest hint of annoyance in her voice she said, "Devin, trust me. This doesn't make sense to ye, yet, but trust me. What we've done today and what we're goin' to do before we get to celebratin' rituals and ceremonies will amplify yahr experiences. Trust me."

Despite the annoyance in Shavon's voice, I felt the sincerity and the absolute depth to her words. I took in a slow, deep breath and gradually let it out with a resigned sigh, "I don't have to like it, but I am here, so I might as well trust you."

An impish smile flashed across Shavon's face, "Ye might as well." With those words, we both turned towards the house.

Alchemy of the Heart: Shavon Sun Cloud
Hidden in Plain Sight

After a quick shower and a scrumptious breakfast, we trudged back out into the yard. We marched back to the spot where we did our morning exercise.

With no preamble as to what was next Shavon said, "Oi'm goin' to put yahr blindfold on again."

I shrugged my shoulders and responded with, "Okay!" I was thinking, "At least I have my shoes on. How can this exercise be any worse than the morning's exercise?"

After Shavon tied the blind fold around my eyes, she said, "For this exercise, we're goin' to go on a wee walkabout. I want ye to see with yahr mind and not yahr eyes."

Like an inattentive student in middle school, I could only respond with, "What?" Even though I could not see Shavon through the blindfold I knew she was smiling that gentle smile she has when she is explaining something to me.

With a hint of playfulness, Shavon offered, "The exercise we're goin' to do is similar to an activity Obi-Wan asked Luke Skywalker to do. An exercise in trusting yahr other senses… but there'll be no blasters to shoot yahr bottom off!"

Alchemy of the Heart: Shavon Sun Cloud

I chuckled. Shavon continued, "Young Skywalker, the blindfold is yahr version of a blast shield. Yahr job is to use yahr other senses to navigate through the obstacles that Oi, Obi-Wan, set before ye!"

With a bit of good-natured whining in my tone I protested, "But I don't even get a light saber, Master Obi-Wan!?"

Shavon, I mean Obi-Wan, snorted, "I don't want ye to kill yahrself or destroy anythin' on yahr first trip through the farm."

I chuckled, "Such as spoilsport!"

Shavon laughed and continued, "Okay Luke, ground yahrself and then head towards me voice. Oi'll gives you a couple of minutes, and then Oi'll start."

Attempting to be a good padawan, I did what I was told. Using the techniques, I had learned for the fire walk, I began releasing the tension from my body and let it go into the earth. I began to slow down my breathing and then sent my awareness out.

I heard Shavon's beautiful, melodic voice sing something that I didn't recognize. It definitely was not in the American top 50 hits of the week! It was beautifully, beautifully haunting.

Throwing caution to the wind, I took my first step towards Shavon. She seemed so far away. I took another, and another, and another. Then boom! Six feet into the lesson I learned about trust.

Alchemy of the Heart: Shavon Sun Cloud

Or more importantly, I learned not to trust Obi-Wan. Like Luke in the Star Wars movies, I was going to get my butt shot at when Obi-Wan was teaching lessons. In my case, it was Shavon taking me over uneven ground. I was not to trust the terrain, or her for that matter! I stumbled because of a rut in the road. I came close, very close, but did not fall.

Shavon stopped her singing and yelled, "I see ye found the rut in the road. Very perceptive of ye!"

I sarcastically chuckled, "Thanks for the warning."

I could sense Shavon smiling, "Yahr welcome." She returned to singing. This time I walked a little slower.

I don't know how long Shavon had me walk around the farm, but it was for a while as she changed songs a few times.

In my mind, I was in the midst of proudfully boasting to myself, "You got this, Devin," when some sort of sixth sense - or voice of God - screamed out to me, "Duck!"

I promptly responded with, "Huh?" and continued to take a step forward, which resulted in my forehead smacking with a resounding thud on what I suspected was a large, low hanging tree branch.

I heard Shavon yell, "Ye all right?" I could tell there was a tiny bit of concern in her voice, but it didn't make my head feel any better.

I replied, "I'll live!" I raised my hands up to find the offending object. Sure enough, my suspicions were confirmed. I walked into a large, low hanging branch. It appeared that my personal awareness skills were not up to par. But my ability to identify the transgressing object after the fact was outstanding.

Her response was, "Yahr sure?"

I retorted, "Yes." I then lowered my hands to continue with the exercise, hoping it wouldn't get any more painful.

With a little gleeful chuckle in her voice Shavon called out, "Watch out for the next branch!"

In spite of the soreness to my head, I responded with, "The annoying part of the whole ordeal was that I got a warning to duck a fraction of a second before I walked into the branch, and I just ignored it."

Shavon gave a half-suppressed laugh, "Next time listen to the warnin'."

I replied indignantly, "Next time I will!"

I heard no further comment from Shavon. Rather, I heard her begin singing again, a rather enchanting song this time. She sounded even further away and off to my left. Carefully, I headed left. I slowed down for the ruts in the road and even managed to find the tree stump that was in my way. I was getting the sense of this exercise.

I walked around the farm for what seemed a rather long time. I was thinking it had to be time for coffee when this voice in my head yelled, "Stop!"

This time I listened. I wanted to put my hands out and feel around for the obstacle that I was pretty sure was in my way, but I didn't! I stood there for a moment trying to visualize what could possibly be in front of me.

Slowly, ever so slowly, a picture formed in my head. We were at the corral. There was a board across my path just below waist height and another one at head height. In my mind, I could picture the solution to my little predicament. If I just lifted my leg and dropped my head at the same time, I would be able to get over and under at the same time.

I was pretty skeptical of this made-up image in my mind, but I could hear Shavon's words echoing through my mind, "At times in our lives, we have to go against our logical mind and go with blind faith."

Well, here I was, figuratively blind and given an opportunity to try going with blind faith. I took in a deep breath in and lowered my head. I deliberately lifted my leg and crossed over what I hoped was a board across the corral and not just a figment of my unbridled imagination.

I was slightly embarrassed as I could just picture Shavon watching me climb over an imaginary board in the middle of a field. Or even worse, I imagined her asking me later on, "What were ye doin' in the middle of the field, Devin?"

I stood up and faced the direction where Shavon was still singing her beautiful song. I walked towards her. She abruptly stopped singing and enthusiastically spoke, "Very well done, Devin. It appears ye found both boards!"

I chuckled, "I wasn't sure if I imagined both boards… But I wasn't going to take any chances."

Shavon gleefully chortled, "Well done, Devin!"

Playfully, I took a deep bow and asked, "Is it coffee time great divine teacher?"

Shavon gleefully laughed, "It could be."

With that, I slid off my blindfold and began walking towards Shavon. She grinned as she said, "Aren't you quite the gentleman? The lads in Oireland wouldn't wait for me… they'd be off to grab their coffee."

Alchemy of the Heart: Shavon Sun Cloud

I grinned, "I could start treating you like the lads do. But I am afraid you would send me home… and much sooner than I would like! If the truth is to be told, I am starting to like your company."

Shavon exploded in mock indignation, "Just startin' to?" She even placed her hands on her hips to accentuate her pretend displeasure. In my humble opinion, it was quite a theatrical production. Worthy of the Irish equivalent of the Oscars, whatever that may be.

Laughingly I replied, "Yup, just starting to! You spend most of your time bossing me around. Lift that, carry that, move that box over there… and even worse, walking me into trees. Not an endearing quality in a woman I must say."

Shavon sarcastically replied, "Not an endearin' quality in a woman? Ye must jest?" with her hands still strategically placed on her hips for emphasis. "I thought ye yanks love strong, dominatin' women!"

"In defense of my fellow countrymen," I boastfully proclaimed, "we like confidence in our women. Not bossy, over-bearing women."

Shavon started walking towards me again. When she finally stood next to me, we couldn't help but burst into peels of laughter. It may not have seemed funny to others, if they would have watched all our exchange, but it sure was amusing to us.

"Let's gather a few things and go for coffee. There's a place Oi'd like to show ye," were her polite directions.

With that, we headed back to the house.

Alchemy of the Heart: Shavon Sun Cloud Digging Deep (er)

Shavon excused herself from the table to head off to the washroom before her meal arrived. This gave me a few moments to reflect on my day. We'd spent the majority of the morning honing my skills of seeing the world through a blindfold. I was feeling pretty proud of my ability. I wasn't sure this ability would be useful in the real world, but I was still damn proud of myself none the less.

Waiting for Shavon to return to the table, what caught my attention was my sudden realization that, for the first time since I met her, I had really noticed her womanly curves as she walked away to the washroom. In my recollection, this was the first time since I'd arrived that she had worn a form-fitting shirt. Was it a coincidence? This was the first time I was keenly aware of the fact that I, Devin Jones, was seeing Shavon as something other than my teacher and friend. I was acutely aware that she was strikingly beautiful and way, way out of my league.

I was startled out of my thoughts by the movement of Shavon's chair and looked up to see her sitting down.

Shavon smiled, "Ye were on a voyage. What were ye thinkin'?"

I opened my mouth to speak a couple times, but I was lost for words. Nothing came out. I was embarrassed to be thinking about how beautiful Shavon looked... and get caught at it. I didn't know how to tell her, or if I should tell her. If I did tell her, how did I tell her without sounding like some kind of sick stalker? I was like a computer program stuck in a logic loop with no way of escaping.

A playful grin splashed across Shavon's face, "Ye were lookin' at me butt, weren't you? Oi know it's a great butt. These jeans make me butt look exceptionally great, don't they?"

I agreed, "Those jeans do make your butt look great!" It was like someone else was in charge of my mouth. This wasn't the Devin I knew from Florida. This was a cooler, calmer Devin. My mouth wouldn't stop, "But the truth is, you are a remarkably pretty woman, and you would look just as beautiful in a monk's robe or a potato sack."

Shavon blushed and smiled at the same time. It took her a few seconds before she spoke, "Devin, we're headin' down one of the most complicated journeys that a single teacher and a single student of the opposite sexes can have. Oi've never had a male student as gifted and as handsome as ye before."

It was now my turn to blush.

Shavon continued, "Part of the journey yahr on will awaken deep sexual energies that ye never knew you 'ad, or that even existed. Ye'll learn to love yahrself and others deeper than ye ever thought possible. Love will also come to mean something entirely different from what ye think love is right now.

Alchemy of the Heart: Shavon Sun Cloud

Devin, Oi loved one of my teachers with all me 'eart, like Oi'd never loved another before. Oi was his student for over two years. Then abruptly one day, he came to me and said, "Our time is done. Oi can teach you no more! You must leave."

It broke me 'eart. Oi cried for weeks after... Oi'd loved this man so deeply and completely. It was unfathomable for me to imagine he could turn me away!

Over time Oi realized he couldn't teach me anymore because Oi was no longer open to the lessons. Oi was blinded by love in the way Oi wanted to receive love, not in the way he was tryin' to teach me about life and spirituality. He'd been right - Oi was no longer teachable.

Oi met him years later, and he said that tellin' me to leave was one of the 'ardest things he'd ever 'ad to do as a teacher! It broke his 'eart, too, but he knew it was the right thing to do.

Devin, Oi don't know what our path looks like in the future. The only thing Oi do know for sure is that we must always tell the truth to each other. We 'ave to be open to sharing our truths, even if we're embarrassed!"

I was stunned, shocked, and almost didn't know what to say. In my uncomfortableness, I laughingly offered, "Well, it was a good thing I didn't ask you anything personal like, "When does your period start?"

Alchemy of the Heart: Shavon Sun Cloud

Shavon smiled, "On Saturday. Oi'm regular like clockwork."

My eyes were now bulging out of their sockets. Before I could respond, Shavon interjected, "Devin, over time, ye'll know more about me than ye may ever want to know, and Oi'll know more about ye than ye know about yahrself. Oi'll know ye better than yahr own mother.

If yahr thinkin' of runnin', now would be a good time to discuss this. We can get ye a ticket booked for home… in a week or so. Oi still need ye for the workshop this coming weekend. Ye can't go home yet!"

Shavon paused to let what she had just spoken settle in, and to allow for our lunch to be served. The universe, once again, had impeccable timing!

The Florida version of Devin wanted to flee. This was way too personal for that version of Devin. But the new, improved, Irish version of Devin knew that no matter how crazy this particular conversation was, he knew that he had to keep this course. That meant he was in store for far crazier and intimate conversations and discussions. He didn't know what the end game looked like, but he knew this was the path.

A new boldness crept into me as I reached my hand across the table and gently touched Shavon's hand, fingers to fingers. Tenderly, I looked into her eyes and spoke from my heart, "I have no idea what the journey looks like, either. But I know that this is the right path, and you are the person I am to learn from. I know this to be 100% my truth. Shavon Sun Cloud, you will not be getting rid of me so easily. I still have much to learn from you."

Shavon smiled and simply said, "And so it is!"

I withdrew my tender touch and replied, "So it is!"

After lunch, Shavon took us for a ride into the countryside. Even if I was placed under extreme torture, I couldn't find the site we eventually arrived at if I was ever asked to find it again. It was something like, go past this village, turn left at a grove of trees down a windy lane, past another grove of trees, past a stone wall, across a stream, down a gully over a bridge, past some houses and then up another windy little path to an abandoned farmstead.

As I got out of the car, I spoke, "I sure hope you know how to get us home. Because to me, we are in the middle of nowhere!"

Shavon playfully looked around, "We are in the middle of nowhere! Very astute of ye!"

I chuckled, "That's why you pay me the big bucks. To pay attention, isn't it?"

Shavon was grinning as she went around to the boot of the car and rummaged around for a few seconds, victoriously emerging with a small bucket.

Alchemy of the Heart: Shavon Sun Cloud

I looked around the farmstead with a sense of bewilderment. I could only ask, "We are not at the beach. I don't think we are building sandcastles. What's with the bucket?"

Shavon responded with, "Follow me, Grasshopper!"

I chuckled, "You have an identity crisis today? Earlier, you were Obi-Wan. Now you are Master Po from the TV series Kung Fu."

Shavon smiled and headed away from the car, "One must use all the tools at her disposal."

Not wanting to be left out of the adventure, I dutifully followed.

Shavon's head was angled steeply towards the ground like she was looking for something. Quickly, I closed the gap and began walking beside her. Inquisitively I asked, "So, what are we looking for?"

Shavon grinned, "Psilocybe semilanceata."

I stammered in stunned response, "A what?"

With a playful twinkle in her eyes, Shavon responded, "Psilocybe semilanceata."

With a just hint of exasperation in my voice, "I caught that we were looking for psilocybe semilanceata. But what is psilocybe semilanceata?"

Alchemy of the Heart: Shavon Sun Cloud

Shavon, still grinning, said, "Oi could play this out for a long time, but Oi won't. Save ye hours of frustration."

I responded wryly, "Thanks."

Shavon continued, "Psilocybe semilanceata are mushrooms. This area is loaded with them."

"Mushrooms?"

"Mushrooms!" was her playful reply. "To save ye from askin' the next question, we're goin' to make a tea with them."

I was now really confused, "I have vaguely heard of reishi mushrooms and their healing properties. But I never heard of psilocybe semilanceata mushrooms. What are their healing properties?"

Shavon stopped searching for mushrooms for the moment and faced me, "Devin, mushrooms 'ave been used for 'undreds of years by Shamans in many countries for many reasons. These particular ones are used for journeying within. They're a tool to help people experience themselves without their egos and to really feel into a concept. The 60's generation did Shamanism a huge disservice by labelling them as magic mushrooms and using them as a recreational drug. Let me assure ye, they are safe and a necessary tool for the path yahr stepping on!

Alchemy of the Heart: Shavon Sun Cloud

I chuckled, "You're the one telling my mom that you forced me into taking shrooms."

Shavon maintained her gaze, trying to decipher my reaction, "Yahr takin' this rather well."

It was my turn to chuckle, "Let's just say, today nothing surprises me. This morning, I was wearing a blindfold… and I am sure I was beginning to see through it or past it.

Then you said that there is a chance I am going to fall in love with you, and if I do, you might have to stop teaching me. I know you are going to start your period on Saturday and now… Now, you have driven me to the middle of nowhere, to a place I couldn't find if my life depended on it, and now we are picking mushrooms. Picking mushrooms that are illegal to have in your possession in the United States.

So, yes, this day is one for the record book. On the weirdness factor, this day is definitely a ten on a scale of one to ten. But does this mean I am ready to abandon you as my teacher? No, I am not ready to do that."

I chuckled and added, "Not before you take me home or I figure out how to get home."

Relief washed over Shavon's face as she pointed behind me, "'Ome is that way." She paused and added, "Sorry, Devin. Today's been a very strange day for ye."

Alchemy of the Heart: Shavon Sun Cloud

We spent the better part of the afternoon searching for shrooms. We filled the bucket to the top. "This will last us a very long time," was Shavon's only comment as we placed our illegal product in the boot of the car.

Robbie Burns said it best, "The best-laid plans of mice and men often go awry. No matter how carefully a project is planned, something may still go wrong with it."

In my mind, we had a great plan - go to the grocery store. Pick up some bread, cheese and some salad fixings and enjoy a nice quiet evening in. Our plan did not include finding three of Shavon's best friends in the same grocery store who were also buying food for supper. As we were all paying for our groceries, I distinctly heard Shavon say in a cheerful voice, "Bring yahr instruments and come on over to the 'ouse. We can cook supper together."

So much for a quiet evening.

Alchemy of the Heart: Shavon Sun Cloud

Alchemy of the Heart: Shavon Sun Cloud
Into the Chaos of Night

On the drive home Shavon abruptly turned to me, almost driving us off the road, "What was Oi tinkin', Devin? Those three never know when to go 'ome!"

I grinned, "The day just keeps getting weirder!"

Shavon chuckled and nodded as she steered us safely back onto the road.

Wanting to beat the trio that was hot on our heels to the house, we sprinted into the kitchen and hastily dropped the groceries on the counter. We had left Shavon's accounting spread all over the kitchen table and floor.

We had just scarcely moved the various piles of papers to locations deemed safe by Shavon before the back door burst open, "We 'av arrived. Let de party begin!" was Aideen's playful, boisterous call.

Daniel had his guitar out within two minutes of arriving. After quickly tuning it, he promptly started singing. I was told it is a famous folk song, Rising of the Moon.

Many tunes later, Jane turned to me and asked, "Can you sin'?"

Alchemy of the Heart: Shavon Sun Cloud

I laughed out loud. The multiple beers were starting to take effect. My standards about what was a proper response with people I barely knew had lowered, "Yes, I can Sin… But I can't sing."

Apparently, Jane was also starting to feel no inhibitions due to the large quantity of wine she had drunk, "Yahr a smart arse aint yah!?"

I smiled, "I can be."

Aideen chimed in, "Well can yahr..." doing her best to emphasize the words, so it sounds like American, "sing?" She laughed at how the word came out.

Before I could answer, the trio of Oirishmen, in a chaotic chorus, attempted to provide their corrected versions of the word 'Sing.' This would have been okay if they hadn't all tried to talk over each other.

Shavon forcefully interrupted the impromptu American speaking class, "Devin, do ye sin' in public? Or are ye a shower and car sin'er?"

I blushed and searched for an appropriate response, "I have been known to sing in the car to the radio. But I have never sung in public or around anyone before, not even my friends."

Jane squealed, "Never?"

I nodded my head, acknowledging that I had never sung in public.

Alchemy of the Heart: Shavon Sun Cloud

"Me Bejasus, we 'av a musical virgin!" Jane explosively announced.

Aideen piped in, "Every Oirishman can sin'. And nearly every Oirishman 'as sung in public. Tiz in our blood. What's wrong witcha bleedin' Americans?"

I grinned uncomfortably, "I didn't want to get teased or beat up, so I didn't sing."

Daniel snorted, "If we didn't sin' we'd for sure get reefed."

Without asking, Jane took it upon herself to get me to sing, "Devin, yahr gonna sin' wid us. Just folly along best ye can."

Daniel picked up his guitar and started singing. The group - minus me - erupted with excitement and boisterously joined in. Daniel sang a verse, and then everyone joined in the chorus. It was a fun, rowdy song called, The Rattlin' Bog.

Once they completed the song, like flies on a fresh carcass they turned on me, "Ye 'ave to join us!"

Shavon pleaded, "Join us."

Inside I was dying a thousand, no maybe a billion, trillion deaths, but like a man on death row who had nothing to lose, I shook my shoulders, stood straight, and said, "Why not?"

Alchemy of the Heart: Shavon Sun Cloud

The group erupted in excited cheers. Shavon yelled, "Wait, Oi 'ave a lyric sheet for ye!" Then scampered off to her bedroom.

We took Shavon's brief absence as an opportunity to drink more beer and eat more food.

I don't remember who cooked what. I do remember that the feast was delicious. I sort of recollected we all took turns chopping, stirring and adding in spices. With that many cooks in the kitchen, it should have been a recipe for disaster. But surprisingly, the food was awesome.

Shavon scurried back with treasures in hand. As she handed me one of the lyric sheets, Daniel picked up his guitar and started the song again. We continued with our drink, and I reluctantly began to sing… very quietly at first, eventually raising my voice loud enough to be heard.

It appeared that with two additional beers in my system, I lost all inhibitions. I was further energized to sing when Daniel joyously hollered, "Ye've a deadly voice, Devin. Untrained, but a deadly voice."

Shavon nodded her head vigorously in agreement, "Untrained, but a very strong voice!"

The night began blurring in my beer-soaked head. Their beer definitely had higher alcohol content than the beer I was used to drinking!

Alchemy of the Heart: Shavon Sun Cloud

We were singing, drinking, eating, then singing some more. At some point, Shavon got out her guitar and additional song sheets for us all. I am not sure when she did this, but it was still dark outside… I think!

Somewhere in the early hours of the morning, we stopped drinking and just sang. It could have been the alcohol talking, but I was in awe. Collectively, I thought we sounded incredible. The four of them harmonized so well together, and well, I was a beginner, so they tolerated me.

The alcohol had made me brave, so I randomly selected a song to sing solo. "I am going to sing," I declared. I handed a sheet with the music on it to Shavon to play for me. They had each sung many, many songs solo, so why not me?

She looked at the song I selected, "Ye sure?"

I shrugged my shoulders, "I don't know the song. Hell, I don't know ninety-nine percent of the songs we sang tonight. So, what the heck is singing one more song I don't know?"

Daniel cheered, "Dat's de spirit!"

As I was to learn many, many times in the future, there is no such thing as random occurrences when the Universe is imparting a lesson upon a person.

Alchemy of the Heart: Shavon Sun Cloud

I had a few false starts, but as I slowly began to sing the song, I started to experience the raw essence of the song. Like a first gentle tingling of a sneeze, ever so slowly at first, gradually building inside of me until I was completely consumed, I became one with the song, or the song was me. There was no difference. We were one. I held no inhibitions. I sang for the pure joy of singing.

As the last lingering words of the song left my mouth, I began to gradually awake from my song-induced trance. As I opened my eyes, I was shocked to see tears streaming down Shavon, Aideen, Jane, and Daniel's faces.

Completely overwhelmed by the experience, we sat in silence for a long time. I was numb and unsure of what their tears were about. I felt exhausted from the whole experience.

It was Daniel that broke the silence, "Devin, dat was absolutely divine. Oi've naw idea 'ow ye did dat. But it was one of de master performances Oi've witnessed in me life."

My heart soared in a sigh of relief as tears filled my eyes. I have never had someone tell me that anything I did was masterful, EVER! I was completely lost for words. I was swimming in emotions. I could only nod my head in appreciation as the tears streamed down my face.

Alchemy of the Heart: Shavon Sun Cloud

Aideen nodded her head in agreement and spoke, "Since we 'av naw 'ope in 'ell av matchin dat, Oi guess 'tiz time for scratcher."

With those unpretentious words, the trio simply got up and prepared to go. They quickly collected their belongings, helped us tidy up a bit and then, after long, lingering, heartfelt hugs and a couple kisses on the cheeks, they were gone.

As the door closed behind them, the house was suddenly quiet, like a house on Christmas morning just before the kids get up. Together, Shavon and I looked at the dishes in the sink and simultaneously said, "Tomorrow!"

We each turned and headed to our respective beds. Exhausted, I fell face-first onto my bed clothes and all.

Alchemy of the Heart: Shavon Sun Cloud

Alchemy of the Heart: Shavon Sun Cloud

A New Day is Dawning

Sluggishly, I returned to consciousness from my alcohol-induced sleep. Ever so slowly I became acutely aware of two things... okay, three things. A throbbing head, a very full bladder, and a tongue the size of the State of Texas!

Like an elephant seal on a soft sandy beach, I struggled to raise my uncooperative body from my bed. Even though I was moving in exceptionally slow motion, it seemed like I was operating at a ridiculously reckless pace for my head to function properly.

As I finally succeeded in propping myself up to an upright position, my head erupted in a resounding, pounding rhythm - much louder than the very last heavy metal concert I had attended not so long ago - adding to the extreme discomfort I was already experiencing.

Excruciatingly slower than my demanding bladder wanted me to move, I began to make my way towards my bedroom door. I felt like a baby learning to walk, taking one tiny wobbly, faltering step forward, followed by another, then another...

The shift to an upright body position exerted additional pressure on my already over-stretched bladder. My sluggish brain suddenly became keenly aware that there was definitely a need for urgency in my movement.

Alchemy of the Heart: Shavon Sun Cloud

As I rounded the corner out of my room, I could see the bathroom door in the distance, like a shimmering mirage. There was something wrong with the picture I was seeing, but my foggy head could not quite grasp what that something wrong was.

I took another step forward. Slowly, an image was forming in my mind, like an old dot matrix printer filling in the picture, one dot and one line at a time. I still couldn't see the picture clearly, but the mist of haziness in my mind was slowly trying to dispel, much like the morning sun heating the ground, causing the morning fog to dissipate.

Then poof! In a flash, the ominous mist that was controlling my mind was obliterated. The picture that instantly formed was a closed bathroom door. This brought the shocking realization that the bathroom was occupied. This spelled massive, titanic-ending disaster! Sheer panic grabbed hold of my entire body and I froze. My mind raced with the frantic thought, "What to do? What to do?"

Then, as if someone flipped a switch inside my brain, the synapsis was activated into overdrive. I was instantaneously at full capacity. I began frantically calculating distances. Was I closer to the bathroom door than the back door? Or was the front door closer?

Alchemy of the Heart: Shavon Sun Cloud

Despite the fact that my brain was now fully awake and calculating distances at speeds faster than the best super computer's maximum capacity, I couldn't decide what to do. The front door and back door were an equal distance from my current location. Full-scale panic was starting to present itself as a viable option.

Then, to every cell in my tingling body's relief, the bathroom door suddenly flung open, and Shavon cheerfully exited with, "Mornin', Devin."

As I raced by Shavon, I may have mumbled, "Good morning," but I can't be sure. I was completely consumed with one thought, one goal… and that was making it to the toilet.

As I left the bathroom, I had the recognition that, despite a night of drinking, I was feeling pretty good.

Well, except for the giant frog that had taken residence in my voice box. I now had a husky, raspy, late-night radio host voice. Apparently, this is a common complaint from non-singers after a night of singing. Shavon told me lemon tea, warm, not hot, would do the trick to set that frog free.

Undeterred by a night of drinking, I was able to eat the hearty breakfast Shavon had made. It was a weird concoction of cooked eggs with a mixture of quinoa and avocados - nothing like any breakfast this previous Florida boy would be having at home! - but it was tasty and filling, nonetheless.

Alchemy of the Heart: Shavon Sun Cloud

After breakfast, we cleaned the house, and put the various piles of accounting and workshop pages back onto the kitchen table where they had been before our supper guests arrived.

Once everything was squared away again Shavon announced, "We're goin' on an adventure. Wear clothes that ye don't mind gettin' smoky. Pack a few layers. We're goin' to be out in the elements for a while. We'll also be stoppin' to pick up some takeaway for later."

Quickly, I changed clothes and packed the small backpack that Shavon had graciously lent me.

I carried two massive wooden trunks, or 'lockers' as she called them, to the car. One went into the boot, and the other went onto the back seat. The trunks were decorated with ribbons and had runes drawn on them. I had to chuckle at the security on the boxes. On the metal loop where a person would typically put a lock, Shavon had just tied a white ribbon.

I also added to the boot a fire kit, shovel, axe, matches, numerous water containers, and refillable water bottles.

Once everything was in the now seriously loaded vehicle, Shavon appeared from the house, and we were off. She offered no preamble about where we were going or what we were going to do. She just got in the car, checked to make sure my seatbelt was fastened, and we were off.

Alchemy of the Heart: Shavon Sun Cloud

We drove in silence for about half an hour. Driving in silence was not uncommon when Shavon was going to deliver one of her workshops... which made me a little perplexed. I knew her workshop schedule, and there were none scheduled for a few days. But I was smart enough to know that Shavon was in teacher mode, so I wasn't going to interrupt her silence.

Abruptly, we pulled into a small roadside store. The weathered sign above the doorway read, 'Woolens and Fine Textiles.' As I was about to undo my seatbelt, Shavon turned and tenderly touched my hand, "Oi'm up to mischief. Oi need ye not to come into the shop. Ye can get out and stretch yahr legs. But Oi would appreciate ye not peekin' in the store."

She hastily undid her seatbelt and was off to the store before I had the time to be offended or stunned. As I slowly got out of the car, I realized that I felt a little hurt. Still, I couldn't help but smile. My teacher was up to 'mischief' and I had no idea what that meant. The last time she was up to mischief she blindfolded me and walked me headfirst into a low hanging tree branch! I could only hope that the mischief she was up to this time would not hurt too much. My head began to throb as a phantom recollection of the incident.

After a few minutes of aimlessly standing around by the car, I spied a bench a little way away. I wasn't sure how long Shavon would take, so I grabbed a water bottle from the vehicle and leisurely strolled over to the seat to sit down.

I was back at the car for my second bottle of water when I heard the shop door open. Shavon appeared in the doorway with a couple of parcels and a huge smile. The packages seemed to be wrapped in burlap and held together with a rope or cord.

I couldn't help but comment, "Based on the width of the smile on your face, we will have to do many workshops to pay for the little bit of retail therapy you just completed."

Shavon snorted, "Maybe!" as she made her way to the car. After gingerly placing the parcels in the back seat, she turned to me, "Ye goin' to waste the entire day standin' around doin' nothin'? Or are we goin' to go on an adventure?"

I laughed as I slipped into the passenger seat, "Sorry to be wasting time."

As Shavon buckled up her seat belt, she playfully responded with, "Ye should be."

I couldn't help but chuckle and smile. "Where to now?" I asked.

Without offering an answer, Shavon started the car, and we were off once again. Where to? I had no idea, but we were off at breakneck speeds!

Alchemy of the Heart: Shavon Sun Cloud

The road sort of looked familiar. My suspicion about where we might be headed was confirmed as we drove by the workshop retreat center that we used shortly after I arrived in Ireland. We roared up to the pub we had frequented more than once. I turned to Shavon, "Am I getting out?"

A naughty grin flashed across Shavon's face, "Of course! Yahr buyin'. I phoned ahead. They have our sack lunch ready."

I was pleasantly surprised that she was letting me buy lunch. It was rare that she let me pay for anything. I was also deeply suspicious. When Shavon was in her teacher mode, there was always a reason for everything she did.

I got out of the car and quickly went inside. There were a couple of patrons in the pub. I thought to myself, "Must be the lunch crowd."

The server must have recognized me because as soon as she saw me, she went back into the kitchen and came out with two brown paper bags. I paid for them and was back in the car in a matter of minutes, unlike Shavon's shopping experience.

I barely got my seatbelt clipped in when Shavon started the car and was off like a rally driver late for the big race.

This time the area didn't look familiar at all. I had a sneaky suspicion we were heading into new territory.

Alchemy of the Heart: Shavon Sun Cloud

After about an hour on the road, we turned off onto a small dirt track and headed into a hilly, well-wooded thicket. After some incredible dirt path driving, we stopped in front of a small gate attached to an old fence.

Shavon turned to me, "Will ye get the gate, please?"

With that, I slipped my seatbelt off, and headed to the gate. The gate had a simple-to-operate latch. The issue was that it was ancient and highly rusted. After considerable effort, I pulled the gate open wide enough for Shavon to drive through. She drove through the opening and stopped the car on the other side of the gate.

It took slightly less effort for me to close and relatch the gate. I jumped back into the car and was about to do up my seat belt when Shavon stopped me with, "Oi'll save ye the effort. There are a couple more gates." With that, she was off again.

As I got out to open the third gate, Shavon casually mentioned to me, "This is the last one."

Shavon moved through the opening and parked along a dense thicket of trees. By the time I had closed the gate, Shavon had exited the car and was now walking towards me. She had a solemn expression on her face, "Devin, yahr enterin' sacred grounds. Yahr one of only a handful of people to know and experience this land."

Alchemy of the Heart: Shavon Sun Cloud

I was taken aback. I didn't really know what to say other than, "Thank you for trusting me and allowing me to experience this land."

Shavon smiled, "Yahr welcome. From here, Oi'll drive the car to the place Oi'll meet ye just up the track. Oi'll need ye to wait here for at least ten minutes, and then ye'll walk at a slow pace to come meet me. Just follow the car tracks. It should take ye about fifteen minutes to walk there. Ye can take a longer time to walk there if ye want. Just not a shorter time. Oi 'ave things to prepare on the other end."

I smiled and nodded my head, "I understand. Take my time here and no speed walking to find you!"

Shavon grinned, "Correct!" With that, she walked back to her car, jumped in, and was off.

I looked at my watch. It was now 1:06 pm. With nothing else to do, I decided to head over and look at the creek.

The creek was beautiful - calendar picture beautiful. I wished my camera was with me and not in the backpack with my change of clothes.

At 1:20 exactly, I started the slow walk towards Shavon. The car tracks were easy to follow, and the dirt track followed parallel along the stream. No fear of me getting lost. That crazy thought made me chuckle because I actually was lost. I had no idea where

Alchemy of the Heart: Shavon Sun Cloud

I was and how to get out of here. I was blindly following a woman I briefly met in another country and was once again blindly following her into the backwoods.

After walking for a little while, I could vaguely hear what I thought was a drum. As I continued walking, I was able to recognize the drum. It was Shavon's hoop drum. As I continued down the dirt path, the drum got louder and louder.

As I rounded a bend in the road, I was surprised to see Shavon in her full ceremonial regalia - her green wool skirt and shawl. I continued towards her. Instinctively, I knew I was to remain silent until she finished drumming.

As I slowly moved towards her, I noticed a few things: the car was nowhere in sight; her hair was wet; there was a small path towards the creek on my left.

I stopped about two feet in front of her. She continued to drum for a few additional moments as I stood before her. With a loud banging crescendo, she stopped.

She affectionately looked me in the eyes and said, "For today's adventure and experience Oi'm goin' to ask ye to leave the mundane world behind ye. Leave the world of Devin and step into a world of the unknown… of things ye know nothin' about. Oi'm askin' ye for yahr complete trust. Do I 'ave yahr trust?"

Alchemy of the Heart: Shavon Sun Cloud

As Shavon spoke those words, I felt utterly at peace and at ease. My heart was whole. Despite a huge lump forming in my throat, I croaked out, "Yes!"

Shavon nodded, "Today, we're goin' to go on an adventure. This adventure will have you experience yahrself in ways ye may have never experienced yahrself before. Are ye willin' to trust me and undertake this adventure?"

I smiled with confidence, "Yes!"

Shavon grinned, "Excellent!" and pointed to the path that I had previously seen, "We're goin' to head down the trail. Ye'll strip down on this side of the stream. Place yahr clothes in the plastic container on this side of the stream, including yahr shoes. Then ye'll quietly enter the stream and wash. Devin, the water is cool, not cold. No sound needs to be uttered! Take care to clean yahrself as a sacred exercise… with reverence. Ensure you wash all of ye. Take as much time as ye need.

Once yahr clean, ye'll find two packages on the other side of the creek. Open the packages and put the clothes on, and then follow the path. Ye'll find me around a fire. Any questions?"

I shook my head, "No!"

Shavon nodded her head, "Good, see ye around the fire!"

Alchemy of the Heart: Shavon Sun Cloud

Shavon turned and headed up the path towards the stream. There was nothing I could do but follow. It was at that point I noticed Shavon was barefoot.

Shavon stopped before crossing the stream and pointed off towards her right, "Place yahr clothes there!" Then she simply lifted her skirt as to not get it too wet and then waded crossed the stream, leaving me to my thoughts.

The container for my clothes was easy to find. Right beside the container was a nicely decorated wooden box with the word "Soap" carved into it. After I stripped down, I caringly placed my clothes and footwear into the container and carefully closed it.

As I stood now stark naked in the woods, I suddenly felt very vulnerable. Here I was lost, and now adding to that sensation of being lost, I was completely naked! Not something the Florida boy would have ever thought he would be doing. Yet here I was!

I picked up the soap and headed to the creek. Not to doubt my teacher, but holy crap, that water was colder than I expected. I think I muttered a tiny, "Shiiit!" as I got my belly wet. That being said, once I was completely wet, the water temperature wasn't too bad.

I was pleasantly surprised that the swimming hole was quite deep, making it easy to get completely soaked. I actually had to come out of the shallow water to soap down my body. After a good scrub, I walked back, carefully placing the soap into the wooden box, and then waded across the stream to fetch my clothes.

I couldn't help but smile. The two bundles on the path looked remarkably similar to the ones Shavon just bought this morning. I picked up the smaller of the two. I began to gently unwrap the bundle, carefully removing the brown material that was inside of the package. The material was wool, and I suspected it was mixed with something else, as it wasn't scratchy like most wool things that I had ever owned. Come to think of it, the only wool thing I owned was wool socks, and they were all not that great. This wool, on the other hand, felt soft, very soft.

As I unfolded the material, I discovered it was a pair of pants, with a note tied to it, "The pants have a draw string in them. The cord that was used as a wrapper for the package is a ceremonial dress belt. Tie it around your waist." I cautiously set the burlap and the cord down on the ground to free up my hands so I could put on my new pants.

After I put on my pants, I cinched in the draw string, reached down, picked up the cord that I had just put down, and strung it through a couple loops that I was pretty sure were belt loops. Then I tied the cord around my waist, not really knowing what knot to use.

Alchemy of the Heart: Shavon Sun Cloud

Without a mirror, all I could do was look down at my new pants. I had to admit Shavon did a great job picking out the pants. The legs were the bang-on right length and they fit nicely. I don't think I have ever owned an earthy, deep brown coloured set of pants. Mind you, I've never owned wool pants either.

Excitedly, I bent down and picked up the other package and slowly unwrapped it, placing the burlap and cord on the ground. The material was brown as well, but a lighter shade of brown. This was some kind of coat, with cape shoulders. I put it on, and it fit very well. I thought to myself, "Job well done, Shavon." I really wished I had a mirror to see what I looked like.

I reached down and picked up both the burlap pieces of cloth that my clothes had been wrapped in and carefully folded them together. I bound the fabric with the remaining cord. I didn't know what to do with it after that, so I just held on to it as I began my way up the path.

I am glad that Shavon had had me walking barefoot before this forest trip, as the path had a few pokey bits on it; my Florida tender virgin feet would have found this path really challenging to walk on. Today it was only slightly uncomfortable to walk on the pathway.

The pathway was rather pretty. As I weaved my way through the forest, I heard many birds that I couldn't identify.

Alchemy of the Heart: Shavon Sun Cloud

The forest did not have much underbrush, so I could see a building with a thatched roof off in the distance.

The path swung me around to what I could now see as the front of the apparently ancient building. It had a straw-thatched roof, and the building's old wooden door was closed.

I could see that Shavon was seated by a nice little fire that burned in a stone-lined firepit in front of the building. On her right side was an old, weathered table much like the ones I saw in the many medieval movies I had watched. Now that I thought about it, this could be the house on the lake that Rob Roy lived in from the movie of his namesake! All that was missing was livestock.

The path I was walking took me directly to Shavon. As I neared the firepit, Shavon stood up from her seated position. I could tell that she was eyeing up her clothing selection. I stopped about five feet in front of her and, without a word from either of us, I turned around slowly to show off my new attire. As I completed my 360-degree turn I grinned and then spoke, "Thank you for the wonderful clothes. I have never worn wool before. It is not even itchy, as I thought it would be."

She beamed, "Yahr welcome. It appears Oi know me sizes."

I dipped my head slightly, "Yes, m' lady it appears you do know your sizes."

Alchemy of the Heart: Shavon Sun Cloud

Shavon nodded her head in acknowledgement. She took in a deep breath. "As ye learn more, we can add more bits and bobs to make it yahr own personal ritual outfit."

Not knowing what bit and bobs would entail I shrugged my shoulders with a slight bit of indifference and replied, "Okay?!" I wasn't sure whether bit and bobs would be important to me, but, either way, I was in!

Shavon spread her arms wide to show me the area, "This whole area is sacred ground. We have a labyrinth, a North American medicine wheel, a place to meditate by the creek, and a sacred circle where we hold group ceremonies. This property was me mother's and has been in her family for generations. Oi maintain it to use for outdoor ceremonies."

Now I had a little clue as to why we were here - some form of ceremony! I deliberately turned around in a full circle to let in the grandeur of the sacred grounds that I stood on.

Suddenly, my mouth felt saltine cracker dry, my lungs felt heavy, and I had a hard time taking in a full deep breath. I felt like I had a large, warm weighted blanket covering and enfolding my whole body. It was as if I could feel the weight of Shavon's entire matriarchal lineage in the air around me!

I must have stumbled or did something out of the ordinary, as Shavon suddenly appeared at my side, "Ye all right, Devin?"

Alchemy of the Heart: Shavon Sun Cloud

I shrugged my shoulders, my eyes cast to the ground, "I don't know, but I think what I am feeling is what I could best describe as the presence of your family lineage."

Shavon moved closer and put her hand tenderly on my shoulder. I don't know how, but even though I could not see her face in that moment, I was pretty sure I could feel her looking at me. No, it was more like looking *into* me.

"Devin, sometimes ye amaze me! The little boy from the middle of nowhere Florida is here experiencin' things that some people have taken years to cultivate and feel." Shavon sighed. I had seen and witnessed that sigh many times before and I knew it as a sigh of wonderment. "Devin, one of the things that make ye so sweet is that ye 'aven't a clue how deep yahr intuition is!"

I smiled as I lifted my head and looked towards Shavon, "Apparently ignorance is bliss!"

Shavon laughed as she gently pushed me away and replied, "Apparently it is." She turned and began walking towards the building. She called to me, "Come on, let me show ye the cottage."

The cottage, as best as I could describe it, was quaint, with a large fireplace taking up most of the wall right of the entrance. I later discovered this wall was on the north side of the cottage. The doorway faced east as you looked out it.

Alchemy of the Heart: Shavon Sun Cloud

There was a small kitchen cupboard painted white, with a sideboard, and a table beside the fireplace. The one-room cottage was filled with two over-stuffed couches on the west side, a bed, and some Celtic tapestries on the walls.

The cottage was simple and very functional. Yet there was a very impressive Celtic fivefold symbol on the floor that looked like it was neatly painted in gold foil. I remembered from previous lessons that the Celtic five-fold symbol represents the five elements of water, fire, air, earth, and the spirit.

Shavon looked at me, "Well?"

I replied, "Well, what? I find it simple and functional. I suspect it is a nice cozy refuge from the regular world."

Shavon smiled, "It is and that's one of the reasons why Oi keep it maintained."

As I looked up to the roof I inquisitively asked, "My only question is, who still knows how to do roofs like this?"

Shavon playfully grinned and replied, "Oi thought everyone knew 'ow to thatch a roof!"

I couldn't help but smile, "Well it appears everyone in the whole wide world knows this, except me! I feel so special."

Shavon chuckled, "There are many ole timers that still know how this is done. Truth be known, roof-thatchin' is makin' a comeback, cause when done right, the roof will last 20 years! Many Oirishmen make a good livin' thatchin' roofs."

Shifting gears, she invited, "Come on outside. I 'ave one more place to show ye."

As the last syllable faded, she turned and headed out the door towards the back of the cottage. I spun around and dutifully followed, carefully closing the door behind me as I exited.

I had to chuckle, since the next item on the grand tour was the pit toilet. Or as North Americans would call it, the outhouse. It was positioned a little way into the bush.

After the quick tour of the outhouse, we walked back to the front of the cottage and stopped at the glowing firepit. Shavon instructed me, "Sit down. Oi'll go get the kettle and we'll 'ave some tea."

I shrugged my shoulders, "Okay."

With that she left and headed back into the cottage. She appeared a few moments later and handed me the kettle. She pointed to a small hand water pump 30 feet from the firepit, and asked, "Could ye fill the kettle, please?"

I nodded my head, "Of course." I grabbed the kettle from her hand and headed to the pump. I pumped the handle only a couple times before water gushed out.

Alchemy of the Heart: Shavon Sun Cloud

I returned to the firepit to discover that Shavon had already set up a metal tent-type structure over top the firepit that would hold the kettle directly over the fire by a metal hook. It took me a second or two to figure out how the whole kettle and hook thing worked, but once I did, I attached the very full kettle to the hook.

I turned around to see Shavon come out of the cottage with another hook and covered pot. "Stew," Shavon explained.

It must have been the perplexed look painted across my face that caused her to comment, "It's frozen. Oi made it weeks ago, knowing we would be out 'ere at some point in time."

"Oh!"

Shavon looked at me after she hung the stew over the firepit, "Let's go for a short walk!"

I happily replied, "Okay!" and with that we were off. She took me to a beautiful, picturesque swimming hole and a labyrinth - something I knew very little about, other than what she shared in her teachings during her workshops.

Next on the tour was a medicine wheel as well as a few places overlooking the stream near what appeared to be another perfect swimming hole to sit and meditate.

Shavon showed me a small storage shed, where the outdoor cooking pots and various assorted tools and implements were stored. I made a mental note of how neat and tidy everything was stored.

At the end of the tour, we found ourselves back at the firepit. Before we sat down Shavon asked, "Would ye get a couple logs from the wood pile and add it to the fire?"

I nodded my head up and down in silent agreement and then proceeded off to the wood pile. I returned a moment later with a log in each hand and added them to the fire.

We spent the better part of the afternoon putting together the dry ingredients for an unleavened bread that we were apparently going to eat a lot of!

The only hint Shavon shared about what we were doing here - or what we were going to be doing - was, "Tomorrow, we're goin' for a short walk. There is a traditional flour mill up the road and we're goin' to mill our own flour. We're runnin' low here at the cottage as well as at 'ome!"

After a delicious supper of stew without meat, and a flat bread warmed in a cast iron pan with butter, Shavon turned to me, "Tonight we're goin' to take a journey into psychedelics. We're goin' to make a mushroom tea for ye, to see how ye react. One of the easiest ways to take mushrooms is by drinkin' them. Mushrooms, for some people, can be a very unpleasant thing when eaten as a first experience, as mushrooms can be hard on the stomach."

I responded, "Mushrooms?"

Shavon smiled, "Yes, Oi brought dried mushrooms like the ones we picked in the field a couple days ago."

Nervously I chuckled, "Can I ask why?"

Shavon's energy shifted to a very calm, compassionate, caring energy. She spoke with a slight hint of teacher, "Devin, Psilocybin mushrooms, or magic mushrooms, are sometimes used as a non-addictive, recreational drug. But a person can still develop a psychological dependency to the experience that the mushrooms provide. Like a warm security blanket, it can provide an escape from the pressures of the mundane world.

What we're goin' to use the mushrooms for is a spiritual journey. Each person that consumes the tea is taken on a journey without the constraints of the ego. This is important, as our ego colors our perception, or concept, of the reality we think we are livin' in."

Shavon grinned, "The non-spiritual explanation is, when we leave the ego at the bus station, the bus ride we're on is not bound by our own limitations."

With uncertainly in my voice, I replied, "This is an example of seeing the world through the eyes of a child, with a sense of possibilities and wonderment?"

Shavon beamed with pride, "Ye were payin' attention in the workshops, Devin!"

Playfully I smiled and made a gesture with my fingers, "Maybe just a little bit."

Shavon continued, "We're goin' to make the tea outside and then go inside the cottage, where it will be dark, to drink the tea. The darkness makes the journey more pleasant, with less sensory overload. Some people can have a difficult time focusin' on objects after drinkin' the tea, so it can cause undue stress and remove ye from the experience of a spiritual journey for the first time!"

Nervously I chimed in, "You are explaining this one to my mom!"

Shavon, with a playful, yet somewhat sinister laugh said, "If she drinks tea Oi won't have to explain it to her, now will Oi?"

Defensively I responded, "Hey, that's my mom!"

We both laughed.

After our peach cobbler, the sun was just starting to show signs of setting. Shavon asked me, "Can ye go into the shed out back and get the container that contains a cuttin' board, a big knife, and a mortar and pestle?"

"Of course!" I replied and scampered off to the shed.

A short time later I returned to the outdoor table exactly as Shavon was exiting the cottage with a basket of things.

Setting the basket on the table, Shavon, turned to me, "As we prepare this tea, let's take a moment to ground."

I let my hands drop to my sides and I began to consciously feel the ground that was beneath my feet.

Shavon continue, "As we go forward tonight, we can be playful and even silly, but let us be aware of our energies. Let us treat the entire evenin' with sacred reverence that will help us keep this a sacred journey.

Let us be aware of whatever feelin' and experiences that come up for us throughout tonight and for the remainder of our time on this sacred land."

Shavon, looked to me and then to the vast fading horizon, "And so it is."

I replied, "So it is."

Shavon turned to the basket with a sense of reverence and began to unload cups, a container of peppermint leaves, a honeypot, and a tea pot with a sieve in the middle of it with leaves in it. She also pulled out of the basket a small burlap bag of what I assumed to be the mushrooms.

When she had unloaded the basket, Shavon reached into the burlap bag and removed a half dozen mushrooms and handed them to me, "They are brittle, yet kind of tough at the same time. We need them cut into chunks so that we can break them down with the pestle."

I placed them on the cutting board I had grabbed from the shed and grabbed the big knife. True to her words the mushrooms were indeed brittle, yet somewhat tricky to cut. By the fourth mushroom I was getting the hang of it.

Once all the mushrooms were cut to Shavon's liking, she took a couple large mushroom pieces and demonstrated how she wanted the rest of the mushrooms crushed into small bits, not too powdery.

It became my job to crush the rest of the mushrooms as Shavon wandered off to put the kettle back over the fire pit.

Shavon came back numerous times to inspect my work. I must have done something right as she offered no comments or corrections.

Once I was done, I turned and screamed, "Shit!!!" Apparently, I was so focused on the job at hand - or Shavon is seriously part cat!

- that she had somehow managed to sneak up behind me and was even standing looking over my shoulder and I was not even aware of it! When I suddenly turned, she was right there in my face. My involuntary scream was at least a sort of manly scream… I mean, screaming, "Shit!!!" How can that not be manly?

Flabbergasted and jittery, I asked, "What the heck?! Why did you do that?"

Shavon grinned a playful but wicked grin, "Oi was seein' how aware ye were."

As my heart rate began to slow down, I managed to respond with, "Apparently, not very aware."

Shavon chortled, "Apparently!"

Still chuckling, Shavon headed towards the firepit, "Oi'll check on the water."

I had nothing else to do so I headed to the firepit and sat down on a bench.

Shavon carefully lifted the lid off the kettle, "The water is ready." She reached over and grabbed the always-present welding gloves. They were used to grab the metal handles of any pots hung over the firepit.

Shavon looked over at me, "Let's go prep the tea and then we can get the water."

Alchemy of the Heart: Shavon Sun Cloud

I did the only thing I could do, which was to shrug my shoulders in agreement, "Okay!" and got up and headed to the outdoor table again.

Once at the table Shavon instructed me, "Take the sieve out of the middle of the teapot and fill it to about the quarter full mark with dried peppermint leaves. Then pour about half of our crushed mushrooms into the sieve."

Once I had completed the task of filling the sieve, Shavon walked back to the firepit and got the kettle of water. She returned carrying the heavy kettle and carefully filled the tea pot.

When the teapot was full, she set the kettle on the table and instructed me, "Wait a full two minutes before adding the sieve into the tea pot, so the water cools off a wee bit. Freshly boiled water can kill some of the effectiveness of the tea."

After what seemed like way more than two minutes Shavon said, "Okay, ye can put the sieve into the teapot."

I carefully did as instructed and Shavon explained, "We'll let the tea steep for about fifteen minutes and then we'll drink it very slowly in the cottage."

Again, all I could do was shrug my shoulders, "Okay, is there anything else we need to do?"

Alchemy of the Heart: Shavon Sun Cloud

A smile slowly spread across Shavon's face, "As a matter of fact there is."

Shavon turned and headed to the cottage, "Follow me!"

Follow is what I did. We walked back into the cottage and pulled out from under the bed a couple small trunks. In the trunks there were blankets and foamies to act as mattresses.

Shavon instructed me, "Take a lot of blankets, as we don't know whether yahr body will be hot or cold as it experiences the mushroom tea for the first time."

When I finished pulling things out of the trunks, Shavon gave me further instructions. "There is a small, ancient, beige suitcase under the bed. Bring that out as well and just leave it in the middle of the room please. It contains all our necessary ceremony gear."

My simple answer was, "Okay!"

Once I had made my little nest, I noticed that Shavon had made a nest directly across from me and was now fiddling with the fireplace in the room.

I wondered if she was preparing for a fire in the fireplace. I casually asked, even though I thought I knew the answer, "Need any help?"

After a couple second pause, she responded as I suspected she would, "Oi got this."

Alchemy of the Heart: Shavon Sun Cloud

I asked the next question on the top of my mind, "What's next?"

Shavon was quicker to respond to this question, "Wash up the cuttin' board, the knife, the mortar and pestle and then put them all away in the shed, where they came from."

I responded, "Okay!" and went outside to clean up. I found the wash basins and carefully added hot water and soap. I quickly had the few items washed and dried and was stowing them away in their containers when Shavon came outside to join me.

Playfully she looked at me, "Damn, Oi didn't wait long enough. Yahr still not done."

I grinned, "That's okay, I will finish up. After all, aren't I the apprentice?"

Shavon replied, "Maybe so but Oi usually don't like to let the apprentice know that Oi'm bein' lazy!"

Grinning as I picked up the container to go back to the shed, I replied, "It is okay, your secret is safe with me!"

In the background I heard Shavon say, "It better be, otherwise somethin' untoward could happen to you." Then I heard her gleeful Irish laugh.

I stowed the container away in its proper place, shut the shed, and returned to the table just in time to hear the cottage door shut. I noticed the teapot, cups, and the rest of the items that were on the table were no longer there.

I glanced over at the firepit to see that Shavon had broken down the fire and scattered the logs already. I took this as an indication that we were done outside for the night. In true Devin fashion, I shrugged my shoulders and headed inside.

Shavon was in the process of lighting some tall candles. She didn't even turn as I entered the room, "Devin, can ye shutter the windows and latch the door?"

The only possible response I could give was, "Okay!" and I set about shuttering the windows and latching the door.

Once this was done, I went to my nest and sat down, waiting for the next set of instructions. I didn't have to wait long.

Shavon made her way to the middle of the room and sat crossed legged next to the beige suitcase. She looked at me, "Devin, can ye brin' the platter that is on the fireplace mantle to me and then come sit down?"

I got up and fetched the ceramic platter. Shavon indicated I should put it on the floor, and I dutifully set it down. Almost immediately a large candle was placed upon it. As I sat down, she said, "The platter's to save the floor from candle wax. Many, many years ago, after a night of ceremony, the floor was covered in wax. Me mother was not impressed, so she bought this platter from a crafty lady down the road, and we've been usin' it for this purpose ever since."

Gazing at the platter she smiled and said, "It's not overly ornate, and not an artistic wonder. But it is divinely practical and heavy enough that it won't get knocked over. If this platter could talk, oh the stories it could tell, Devin. The stories it could tell!

I grinned, "I suspect that is so true!"

Shavon looked at me, "Tonight we're goin' to keep our ceremony simple. We're goin' to use what many people believe is a North American tradition. However, it is not unique to North Americans. Many of the indigenous peoples around the world use the four directions in their spiritual practices. Oi suspect not many people know about the other cultures as they've not been as quick to share their traditions as the North Americans were. Or perhaps we 'aven't spent enough time with them to earn their trust.

Regardless, we're goin' to use the four directions. Ye may have 'eard me use these in previous workshops."

I nodded my head in acknowledgement. Shavon simply grinned, "Good," and continued with her explanation of the coming ceremony.

"After the openin', we'll sip our tea and Oi'll teach ye a couple medicine songs. At some point in the evenin' the tea will take ye on a journey. Wherever it takes ye, when yahr journey comes to an end, we'll call the four directions to end the ceremony and go to sleep. Any questions?"

I couldn't think of any questions other than, "What's the honey for?"

Shavon smiled, "To help mask the taste. Some people find the taste of the tea a bitter drink and hard to swallow. The honey makes it more palatable."

Shavon made a face and swore, "Shit, I forgot the ginger!"

I wondered, "Should I be worried?" What I said out loud was, "Ginger?"

"For those with sensitive stomachs ginger helps to diminish the indigestion." Shavon locked eyes with me, "Oi'm trustin' yahr stomach will be okay. If not, we'll deal with it at the time."

I was definitely getting worried, now! I nervously chuckled, "Just remember, you are explaining this to my mother!"

She laughed, "Okay!"

With that, she reached over and poured a cup of tea and handed it to me, "I suggest tryin' a little honey. Ye can add always add more if ye want, but you can't remove the honey after ye've added it to yahr tea!"

Alchemy of the Heart: Shavon Sun Cloud

As I reached over and took the teacup from Shavon I grinned, "Good point."

I dipped a spoon in the honey pot and carefully added a little dallop of honey.

Shavon poured herself a tea and she, too, added a small dallop of honey. Then she set the honey pot to the side.

I saw her body physically straighten and felt her energy shift to that of a leader. I knew that was my signal that she was about to start the ceremony. I had witnessed this magical change a couple times before.

Shavon spoke in a kind, loving way, "Let us stand facin' the fireplace, facin' north."

I stood and faced the fireplace as requested.

I don't know if it was my imagination, but her accent appeared to have suddenly gotten thicker as she spoke, "In many ancient, religious traditions, it's customary to brin' a service o' worship or celebration by callin' on de four directions.

This is a way o' symbolically invitin' all of creation to be present and take part in de festivities. Fahr this ceremony, Oi'm going to use a version of de North American First Nations directions that me teachers taught me. Ye may, or may not, 'ave 'eard dese. When we do other ceremonies on this land, Oi'll use de more traditional

Alchemy of the Heart: Shavon Sun Cloud

Celtic callin' in o' de directions, but fahr this evenin' let's honor yahr roots, Devin."

I shrugged my shoulders with my usual, "okay."

Shavon continued, "This evenin', we, too, want to invite de whole o' creation to be with us 'ere and now."

Shavon raised her arms, turned and pointed her body to the doorway. I mimicked her.

"Oh, Great Spirit o' de East, we turn to ye where de sun comes up, from where de power of light and refreshment come.

Everythin' dat is born comes up in dis direction - de birth o' babies, de birth o' puppies, de birth o' ideas, and de birth o' friendship.

Let there be de light.

Oh, Spirit o' de East, let de color o' fresh risin' in our life be glory to ye."

Shavon directed me, "Devin, turn to the South." I turned a quarter turn to the right.

"Oh, Great Spirit o' de South, spirit o' all that is warm and gentle and refreshin', we ask ye to give us dis spirit o' growth, o' fertility, o' gentleness.

Caress us with a cool breeze when de days are hot.

Alchemy of the Heart: Shavon Sun Cloud

Give us seeds dat de flowers, trees, and fruits o' de earth may grow.

Give us de warmth o' good friendships.

Oh, Spirit o' de South, send de warmth and growth of yahr blessin's."

Shavon directed me, "Devin, turn to the West." I turned a quarter turn to the right.

"Oh, Great Spirit o' de West, where de sun goes down each day to come up de next, we turn to you in praise o' sunsets and in thanksgivin' fahr changes.

Ye're de great colored sunset of de red west, which illuminates us.

Ye're de powerful cycle which pulls us to transformation.

We ask fahr de blessin's o' de sunset.

Keep us open to life's changes."

Shavon directed me, "Devin, turn to the North." I turned a quarter turn to the right to face the fireplace once again.

"Oh, Great Spirit o' de North, we come to ye and ask fahr de strength and de power to bear what is cold and harsh in life.

We come like de buffalo ready to receive de winds that truly can be overwhelmin' at times.

Alchemy of the Heart: Shavon Sun Cloud

Whatever is cold and uncertain in our life, we ask ye to give us de strength to bear it. Do not let de winter blow us away.

Oh, Spirit o' Life and Spirit o' de North, we ask ye fahr strength and fahr warmth."

Shavon raised her arms up high above her head, "Oi pray that yahr 'eart, mind, soul, and spirit will not forget to look upward this day, to the One who is so much greater than we are. We ask Father Sky for his blessin' as we embark on this ceremony and ritual adventure tonight."

Shavon then bent down and touched the floor, "We ask that Mother Earth blesses everythin' we do tonight and everythin' in the following days. We trust that we'll honor and be in reverence of our Mother Earth."

Shavon then placed her hand on her heart, "We ask for blessin' that all that we do this evenin' will be true and from de Spirit o' God, de Spirit o' Christ, de Holy Spirit, whoever or whatever divine power ye know to be true that dwells within ye."

"A-ho!" was the final incantation of her blessing. I knew to respond with, "A-ho," meaning, "I hear you and I recognize the words you have spoken."

Shavon indicated for me to sit down, and I did as I was asked. She sat, too, and raised her cup, "Drink Devin, even if it seems cold. Ye don't want to guzzle the tea down because if ye do the

Alchemy of the Heart: Shavon Sun Cloud

medicine may hit ye like drivin' yahr head into a brick wall. The first time we take tea, we want to dance with it, feel its gentle sensations so the effects don't steam roll over us!"

I nodded my head in agreement and took a tentative sip of the tea. Instantly the bitterness rushed to all the muscles in my face like a runaway freight train. There was no hiding the fact that I thought the tea was bitter, and to add to the effect I coughed. Quickly I recovered and squeaked out, "I think I want more honey."

Shavon laughed heartily at me, "Yahr doin' better than Oi did the first time Oi tasted it. Me face twisted up in horrible expressions for - no lie - ten minutes straight."

I reached over, hurriedly grabbed the honey and the spoon, and quickly added an additional, healthy dallop of honey. After a quick stir, I put the cup to my lips and it was a tiny bit better, but… "I don't think all the honey from the honeypot would stop it from being bitter! But I think I am going to be able to drink it."

Shavon replied, "Good."

I reached over and put the honeypot back, then took another sip of the tea.

Shavon chuckled, "Slow down, sailor."

I looked over at her incredulously, "Really?"

She laughed, "Not really but the look on yahr face was worth it!"

Alchemy of the Heart: Shavon Sun Cloud

Shavon, still smiling, asked, "Ave you 'eard of Deva Premal?"

I shook my head.

"No?" Shavon continued, "She is famous for singin' Sanskrit chants. Her singin' is beautiful."

I shrugged my shoulders, and said, "Okay!"

"Instead of me tryin' to teach ye Gaelic, or traditional Oirish folk songs, we'll learn some o' de more common English songs that can be used in ceremony to start with."

I wondered out loud, "Why?"

Shavon didn't laugh at my question. "That, my dear Devin, is a great question. Music transcends all languages. Even if ye don't know the words, ye know the feelin' behind the music. Music reaches the soul, which is why first nation peoples always used music in their teachin' and in healin' ceremonies. Music inspires and reaches our souls beyond what our egoic self lets in!"

Shavon reached down and took a hold of her cup, waiting for me to do the same. We raised our cups in unison, "Cheers." Again, in unison we took a sip of tea.

Once we set our cups down Shavon continued, "After ye go 'ome, if ye want to continue with yahr spiritual journey, Oi would ask ye to continue singin' and to take up music lessons, either a traditional flute or guitar. Yahr choice of instruments, Devin, but being musical does help in experiencin' the teachin's deeper."

I chuckled, "Apparently, when I came across the pond, I didn't read in the fine print that music lessons are required."

Shavon chuckled, "It's in the contract appendices. Ye must have missed it."

I snorted, "Must have."

We both took another sip of tea. Shavon continued, "Oi'm goin' to teach you a song by Deva Premal called, 'All Is Welcome Here'." She looked around her nest, apparently looking for something.

Before I could ask her what she was looking for, she stood up ever so slowly and walked over to the bed. She moved the piles of blankets around before she gleefully spied what she was looking for. She happily pulled her guitar from a case that had been camouflaged in the deep pile of blankets. She sat on the edge of the bed while she expertly tuned her guitar.

Once she had it in tune, she came back over and sat down in her little nest.

As I took a sip from my cup, I must have made another face or something because Shavon instantly had deep concern written all over her face. She asked me, "What's wrong?"

Alchemy of the Heart: Shavon Sun Cloud

I was struggling to figure out what I was experiencing. "I… My… My face feels hot, and my ears feel like the sensation you get when you hold seashells up to your ears. Kind of full and you think you can hear everything."

Shavon chuckled, "Ye react fast. We aren't even done the tea and yahr already feelin' the effects." She squiggled around and got herself comfy.

Once she found the right spot, Shavon picked up her guitar and strummed a few cords. She then began to play a song and started to sing, "Broken hearts and broken wings… Bring it all, bring everything… Bring the song you fear to sing, All is welcome here." [1]

She sang the song again. She sang each of the lines a couple more times and then asked me to join in.

After a few tries I got the words and even the right timber. My voice was a little wobbly and pitchy, because I was still not used to the idea of singing out loud in front of someone else, let alone trying to sing with someone who has an incredibly beautiful voice. And - a big AND – I was singing without alcohol to calm my nerves! I was without liquid courage, unlike the first time I sang with Shavon and the group.

---

[1] 'All is Welcome Here', song by Deva Premal and Miten

Alchemy of the Heart: Shavon Sun Cloud

We had sung the whole song a couple times when I just abruptly stopped. Shavon stopped playing and inquisitively asked me what I was experiencing.

I leaned towards Shavon and conspiratorially whispered, "Is it normal to hear the blood in my body course through my veins?"

Shavon leaned in towards me and matched my tone, "For some people it is normal. Apparently, yahr one of the chosen ones!"

My eyes popped open, like a strobe from a camera flash. I felt almost giddy to be amongst the chosen ones, "Really?"

Shavon leaned even closer to me and hushed her voice even more. As she spoke, I knew in my heart that she was sharing the secrets of the entire universe with me. What she was sharing with me, she had told no one else before. I was the chosen one. My heart was pounding in my chest with excitement.

Shavon put her finger to her lips indicating for me to be quiet. I shrunk down, making myself small. I thought if I was small, I would make less noise.

Quietly, in a hushed whisper Shavon spoke. I was holding my breath. "Devin, this is just the beginnin'. Put yahr seatbelt on. We're…"

Alchemy of the Heart: Shavon Sun Cloud

From my scrunched ball of existence, I reached over, trying to find a seatbelt. My arm was flailing wildly and in a mildly panicked voice, I managed to squeak out, "I can't find the seatbelt!"

Shavon took in a slow deep breath before she carefully and tenderly responded, "That's okay, Devin. Oi got it for both of us."

The panic that had been incrementally building up inside of me gradually began to vanish. Shavon had us. She was holding onto the seatbelt, and I felt safer. Much safer truth be told.

Little did I know that this innocent little thought would cause me years of good-natured teasing!

Slowly I sat back into the comfort of my nest, knowing that Shavon was holding onto the seatbelt to keep us safe.

I reached up to my right ear and rubbed it, trying to remove ear wax that I was pretty sure had suddenly filled my ears; why else would there be a sensation of them being suddenly plugged?

I heard Shavon move her guitar. Instinctively I looked over to her. My sudden head movement caused a wave of nausea to wash over me. But that was the least of my worries! My vision was now blurred by giant, colorful, whirling gears of various sizes. The gears were spinning in multiple directions in full 3-D, some in a clockwise direction, and others counter-clockwise.

Alchemy of the Heart: Shavon Sun Cloud

I could hear the gears spinning, even though my ears were completely plugged now. It was like my ears were completely underwater.

As the gears spun, I could feel the temperature of my body rise. I could feel myself burning up. I could feel myself melting.

As I felt the sensation of my body melting, I could see the gears melting as well.

In my drug-induced state, I knew that I had to take off my clothes or I would melt like the witch in the movie the 'Wizard of Oz'. I could hear the witch yelling repetitively, "I am melting, melting!" which added to my sense of panic.

In my mind, I tore off my clothes, but it offered only momentary respite from the searing heat. Frantically my mind searched for a solution. Then it hit me like a bolt of lightning, a desperate flash of inspiration… the creek!

With that thought, I sent my body careening towards the creek. I sensed my body running over the well-worn path to the swimming hole. I did not slow down, even as I felt parts of me sliding off like wax on a pillar candle.

With a resounding splash I was face first in the swimming hole.

The creek offered some relief from the intense heat. Frantically, I waded back to the shallower waters near the shore where I quickly examined my body to ensure that I was whole and intact, and that no part of me had melted off.

I let out a huge, audible sigh of relief when I could see that none of me had melted off.

Then I heard a voice in the distance, "Ye all right?" It took a few seconds before I recognized it as Shavon's voice.

I stuttered out my response, "Yes, I was just making sure nothing had melted off my body, because my body was melting from the intense heat in the cottage."

As an afterthought, I added, "Are you okay?"

I heard Shavon giggle, "Oi'm okay. Glad nothin' was melted off."

Excitedly I replied, "Me too!"

In my mind's eye, it appeared that my body parts stopped sluffing off, but the ever-present sensation of intense heat remained. If this was manopause, I was not impressed.

As I stood in the creek, I could feel the temperature of the water rise. Hysterically, I leapt into the deep end again and plunged my head underwater, desperately trying to cool off before the water got too unbearably hot!

As I was underwater, I opened my eyes. I could suddenly see the fish in the creek looking at me, pleading with me, "Stop the heat!

Alchemy of the Heart: Shavon Sun Cloud

Stop it! You are boiling us alive!" I could hear their thoughts; they were talking with me! No, they were pleading with me, "Stop this foolishness. It is time to stop blaming everyone one else for all the things wrong in your life. It is time to be 100% accountable for your life."

I opened my mouth and spoke to the fish, "What do you mean?"

The larger of the fish responded, "When you stop blaming everyone else and start learning from the experiences you have had, you take back control of your life. You must understand that situations that are less than ideal are always going to appear in your life... Like your fire walking incident."

I was mortified, "How the hell did you know? A fish thousands of miles away from my home in Florida knows about my fire walking accident?"

The fish calmly responded, "We are all connected. There are no secrets in the universe and when you understand we are all one and we are all connected, your life will become easier."

The large fish paused and then continued, "When you begin to accept the possibility that life happens for you and not to you, your life changes. If you would NOT have burned your feet at the workshop, there is a particularly good chance you would not have met Shavon, and you would not be here!"

Alchemy of the Heart: Shavon Sun Cloud

I was struck by the absurdity of the fish's statement yet had to admit that it was absolutely true. If I hadn't burned my feet, I would never have been here in Ireland talk to a fish underwater. So, me burning my feet had been a blessing in a way!

I was in the midst of asking the scholarly fish another question, when I was unceremoniously and rudely plucked from the water.

I came to the surface annoyed and aghast that Shavon had reached down, put her arm across my chest and roughly pulled me out. How could she do this to me as I was right in the middle of a conversation? With a real sense of annoyance clearly etched across my face, I demanded, "Why did you do that? I was in the middle of a conversation with an incredibly wise fish."

Yes, it would be an exceptionally long time before I would live that particular line down.

Shavon with a sense of 'oh brother' said, "Well excuse me!" and promptly pushed me back into the water. As my face hit the water, I began frantically searching for the wise ole' fish. I swam left, then swam right, but the wise ole' fish appeared to have vanished.

Like a 5-year-old boy whose friends had left him to go play somewhere else, I surfaced with a pouty, "He's gone!"

Shavon was quick to respond, "Did yahr friends leave ye, Devin?"

Alchemy of the Heart: Shavon Sun Cloud

The little hurt boy in me responded with a pouting lower lip, "Yes."

Shavon heartily laughed, reaching over to slam my head back into the water. The last words I heard were, "Maybe ye should go find them!"

After a few seconds I felt her release the back of my head. Apparently, she was not too seriously intent on drowning me today!

I swam a few feet away from Shavon then unhurriedly turned and gradually floated to the surface, my eyes, nose, and mouth just breaking the surface of the water.

Suddenly, I was very aware of the coolness of the water, and the sensation of water over my entire, apparently naked body. My hands quickly verified, that yup, I was somehow naked. I looked over at Shavon who was apparently still in her ceremonial robes. She was astonishingly beautiful standing there in the creek, highlighted in the little bit of the moonlight.

I didn't know what to think, do, or say. So, I asked the only thing that made sense to me, "You, okay?"

Shavon smiled and tenderly chuckled, "The better question is, are ye?"

Alchemy of the Heart: Shavon Sun Cloud

I went quiet for a few moments before I responded, "I think so. I now know I am completely naked, in the swimming hole and I have had a very in-depth conversation with a very scholarly fish. But *how* I got naked and how and why I am in the swimming hole are yet to be pieced together."

I followed that statement with a rather embarrassed question, "I didn't do anything to hurt you or do anything untoward, did I?"

Once again, Shavon laughed, "Oh, Devin. Once ye decided ye needed yahr clothes off, ye took them off, folded them all nicely, and placed them in a pile. Then ye gave me a bit of a scare because ye took off like a scared rabbit toward the swimmin' hole. No matter how fast Oi ran, ye were faster."

My soul let out a sigh of relief that I had done nothing untoward. Drug induced state or not, I would not have forgiven myself if I had hurt her in anyway.

I grinned, "I suspect you thought I was drowning when you pulled me up out of the water?"

Shavon responded with, "Oi did."

I grinned, "I don't think I was at that point. But I probably could have, so thank you very much for your help."

It was Shavon's turn to grin, "Oi wasn't goin' to be the one to tell yahr mother that I let her boy drown."

Alchemy of the Heart: Shavon Sun Cloud

I chuckled, "Great idea!"

I must have made a face again or something because Shavon asked, "What's up?"

I could feel my face become flushed with embarrassment, "I don't know the appropriate decorum to extract myself from the water."

My comment caused Shavon to have a huge, heartfelt belly laugh, "Devin, ye don't 'ave to worry about runnin' around naked with me now. Oi've seen ye in full light and not just some meagre moonlight like now. The best way for ye is to head on home and let me get a towel out o' de cottage."

With that, I shrugged my shoulders okay and headed to the shore. I waited dripping wet on the bank for Shavon to extract herself from the swimming hole.

On the way back I asked her, "How long was I under the influence of the mushrooms?"

She guessed, "Forty minutes to an hour."

Once we reached the cottage yard, I went straight over to the firepit. The fire offered a few degrees of warmth to this naked, shivering soul. Just before Shavon entered the cottage she called back to me, "Maybe add a log or two?"

I heartily agreed, "Okay!" and darted off to the wood pile. By the time I returned with an armful of wood and placed it on the fire,

Alchemy of the Heart: Shavon Sun Cloud

Shavon was beside me with a towel, "Dry off and Oi'll go back in and get yahr clothes."

I looked at her and offered a sincere, "Thank you."

She replied with a smile and, "Yahr welcome!" then promptly headed back to the cottage.

When Shavon returned with my leggings and shirt, she was wearing a dry set of clothes herself. The wool clothes seemed comfortably warm as I slipped them back on. Thank goodness the logs I had put on the fire were now coming to life and offering up real warmth. I was still barefoot, but I was warming up.

Shavon said, "Oi'll put the kettle back on!"

I grinned, "Sure, but I may just have a plain mint tea!"

It was Shavon's turn to chuckle, "That's probably best." With that she was off to fetch the kettle and water.

Once the kettle was on over the firepit it was my turn to talk, "Apparently, I am one of the people that experiences heat when I take the medicine."

Shavon responded, "Apparently!"

I asked, "Your experiences, you get hot or cold?"

Shavon frowned, "Mostly cold, but a few times Oi've 'ad intense heat like yahr experience. It seems most people get cold, that's

Alchemy of the Heart: Shavon Sun Cloud

why we 'ave so many blankets in the cottage." Then Shavon laughed out loud, "Oi'll say this. Yahr experience is a first! Oi've never 'ad anyone say they were communing with a fish."

I chuckled and offered up as further description, "It was a scholarly fish. Not just an ordinary fish."

As Shavon bowed, she quipped, "Oi'm sorry, please forgive me. Oi've never 'ad anyone commune with a SCHOLARLY fish before."

I laughed again, "You are forgiven this one time!"

Shavon's energy shifted. She asked with a hint of curiousity, "What did our scholarly fish share with ye?"

My energy shifted as well, "He was trying to explain the lesson that things happen for a reason and when you look upon them as they happen *for* you and not *to* you, life can take on a different meaning. As an example, I was pissed that I burned my feet in the fire walk, but had I not burned them, we would not have met in the circumstances that we did, and we would not be experiencing what we are experiencing as it is showing up now!"

Shavon clapped her hands together excitedly, "Very good. The fish was an excellent teacher."

I corrected her, "The scholarly fish was an excellent teacher."

Alchemy of the Heart: Shavon Sun Cloud

Shavon grinned, "Forgive me! The scholarly fish was an excellent teacher."

We both laughed in agreement, "Yes he was!"

The kettle boiled and re-boiled a few times as I shared my experience with mushrooms. We laughed many times about me coming up spitting, sputtering and mad because Shavon had interrupted the scholarly fish talking to me!

After a long while, we finally decided to call it a night. We cleaned up the outdoor kitchen area again and then crawled into our respective nests in the cottage.

The morning seemed to come early. I was grateful I appeared to have no residual effects of the mushrooms… but I couldn't remember if we had called in the four directions again to close the ceremony. When I checked in with Shavon later that day, she said, "Devin, we did close the circle. It appears the mushrooms really worked magic on yahr memory."

We both took our time to crawl out of our comfy nests. Eventually our stomachs drove us from our beds and out to the kitchen.

Shavon said, "Breakfast is simple this mornin'. Fresh bread, jam, cheese, and tea."

I got the fire going as Shavon scurried about collecting the fixings for breakfast. I put the kettle on while she whipped up the bread mixture and plopped it in a giant frying pan that hung over the fire pit.

Hot fresh bread is heavenly. I liked it even more because we ate it right off the frying pan - less dishes for me to wash.

During breakfast I broached the subject that had been on my mind since we first got here, "In the past you have had people here for ceremony. Are we doing one anytime soon?"

Shavon chuckled, "As a matter o' fact, we're doin' one this comin' weekend."

I sputtered, "Really?"

Mockingly Shavon replied, "Remember, Oi'm the teacher. Oi don't have to tell ye everythin'."

I pretended to look at a watch that I wasn't wearing, "It is not even 9:00am and you pull the 'I'm the teacher' line already!"

Shavon, giggled and wagged a finger at me, "Oi just didn't want ye to forget it, Mr. Smarty Pants."

I playfully shook my finger back at her, "I won't forget that you are the teacher, Ms. Witchy Poo."

Shavon launched into full, gut-wrenching belly laughter. I had never heard her laugh so heartily before. When she was able, she sputtered out, "Oi've been called a witch, a bitch… But never

Alchemy of the Heart: Shavon Sun Cloud

Witchy Poo!" When she uttered the words 'witchy poo', she was again engulfed in another round of belly laughter.

The sad part was I didn't find the term Witchy Poo funny, but Shavon's laughter was contagious. It didn't take long before I, too, was caught up in a spontaneous bout of side-splitting belly laughing. I wasn't doubled over on the ground laughing, but my belly was hurting.

After a few long, drawn-out moments, I had to go and hide around the cottage so I wouldn't see Shavon. I was really only laughing because she was laughing. I figured if I didn't see her, I wouldn't be laughing.

As I was around the backside of the cottage trying to regain my composure, I overheard the cottage door open and close. I could clearly hear Shavon attempting to get her laughter under control in the cottage. I grinned as I proceeded to walk back around to the firepit to clean up the area.

From the outdoor kitchen area I could still hear intermittent movement in the cottage and the occasional chortle of laughter. In spite of the occasional distraction, it didn't take me long before I had the outdoor kitchen area all cleaned and things put back to where I thought they came from.

I glanced proudly around at my handy work, then with a shrug and thoughts of, "What's next on the list to do?" I wandered off to the wood pile. I remembered where the axe was stored and decided to try my luck at chopping wood. It went remarkably well.

A long time – and I mean a very long time - later Shavon exited the cottage as if nothing had happened. She found me at the wood pile and beamed her flashy, everything-is-alright-and-trust-me-completely-because-I-know-best smile and said, "Let's go for a walk!"

Dutifully I agreed, "Okay!"

I piled the wood I had just split and then put the axe back into the shed. With that we headed back out behind the cottage and off onto a little trail into the woods.

I turned to Shavon, "Is it me or does the world seem brighter this morning?"

Shavon smiled a big, the-boy-noticed kind of smile and replied, "The days after mushrooms always seem brighter. Nature's colors seem more vibrant to me as well."

I nodded my head in agreement, "Yes, the Irish countryside does seem a little greener to me today… if that is at all possible."

It wasn't too long before we came to a small man-gate. We opened it, went through, closed it, and then continued walking down a small gravel road, much the same as the one we drove down to get to Shavon's property. On the road, I noticed what I assumed were hoof prints and the tell-tale signs of animal droppings. My animal husbandry was lacking so I was unsure if it was horse or cow droppings everywhere. I opened my mouth to ask Shavon, "Are these…?"

Shavon grinned and I was instantly deafened by a high-pitched, shrill whistle. Her whistle was much like the loud whistling you hear on a construction site. She followed this with a very un-lady-like bellow, "Beauty! Come on! Beauty!"

With eyes wide open in mild shock, I turned to ask, "Why did you do that?" but even before the words escaped my mouth, I could feel the ground begin to tremble and I heard crashing off in the bush.

Soon there was a thunderous pounding coming from all directions around us. My eyes must have been as big as saucers when I saw the first horse come crashing out of the bush. My eyes kept getting bigger as I saw more and more horses coming from all directions. I am no horse person, but even this city boy from Florida knew that these were damn big horses, and they were bearing down on us pretty damn fast! I now knew why the Calvary in the middle-ages scared the hell out of the common soldier; I just about wet my pants!

Alchemy of the Heart: Shavon Sun Cloud

Just as I was about to bolt, I felt Shavon take my hand, "Stand still, Devin! If ye move, we risk gettin' 'urt as the 'erd tries to avoid us at full speed. By nature, an 'orse will try to avoid ye."

I was not Catholic, but I felt like praying! As the horses kept bearing down on us, I was keenly aware that they knew Shavon, but not me. I envisioned them trampling me to death to protect her! It also appeared they were not going to stop. I closed my eyes, "Oh, God! Please don't let it end this way! I still have so much left to do!"

When I opened my eyes, I felt like Moses must have after he parted the seas. Right after my prayer, the horses instantly, and in synchronicity, slammed on their breaks, coming to a skidding stop on their hind haunches. There was dust and gravel everywhere. The few horses that could not stop easily parted right in front of us and gracefully went around us. They slowed down, turned, and calmly proceeded to trot back to us. I don't know how many horses surrounded us, but there were a lot of them, and they were huge!

Shavon commented, "They're Oirish draft 'orses. They're all retired work 'orses. This land is a refuge for unwanted drafts." She pushed her way into the heard, coming to stand next to a beautiful, chestnut, muscular horse. "This one is Beauty, the only stallion in the group. He 'as a bit o' attitude; he knows he's a damn good-looking 'orse. He may be vain, but he loves people, and he comes when you call 'im. Where he goes the 'erd follows."

Alchemy of the Heart: Shavon Sun Cloud

It was a good thing Shavon was still holding my hand as I was violently thrown forward by an energetic head butt to the middle of my back. Miraculously, I was able to stay standing. Shavon laughed, "That's Molly. She's the matriarch of the 'erd, and she wants some attention. Ye better scratch her 'ead and ears or ye'll never be her friend."

I was feeling rather intimidated. Nervously I turned to Shavon, "How?"

Shavon chuckled, "City folk." She reached up and started to scratch Beauty's head and ears. I did my best to imitate Shavon's moves. I felt better when I sensed Molly leaning into the scratches. I knew I was doing something right.

I heard Shavon call out to me, "Ye better get the left 'and goin' if you don't want another 'ead butt! There are other 'orses that want lovin'."

I don't know how long we stood in the herd scratching heads and quietly talking to each horse. Maybe it was the awareness generated by the mushrooms; as I looked into each horse's eyes, it was like I could see their soul. I could feel their love and their pain.

When the last horse slowly walked away, I could feel tears streaming down my face. I had no idea when the tears started and I was unashamed of the salty water streaming down my face.

Alchemy of the Heart: Shavon Sun Cloud

Shavon silently walked over and gingerly took my hand again. Tears were streaming down her face, too. Without saying a word, Shavon gently tugged on my hand indicating the direction we were going to walk towards.

We ambled along, each lost in our own thoughts for a couple hundred yards when I broke the silence. Tearfully I shared, "I will carry that experience with me for the rest of my life. I have no words for the humbling experience other than…" I turned and unabashedly kissed Shavon tenderly on the cheek, "Thank you!"

She smiled and then we turned and resumed our walk down the road, still holding hands.

I could see various members of the herd. They hadn't dispersed very far and their presence helped further embed the feelings and sensations of the truly remarkable experience I had just had.

We walked for a couple hundred more meters before we turned onto a small, quaint, non-descript road. In the distance I could see a small stone building.

As we got closer, I asked, "Is this the mill?"

I got excited when Shavon answered, "It is."

It appeared we were coming at it from the backside, as I could hear water flowing from the other side of the building, "Is that the same creek as the one flowing on your property?"

Alchemy of the Heart: Shavon Sun Cloud

Shavon nodded her head and replied, "It is."

As we arrived at the building Shavon said, "Liam doesn't appear to be 'ere today. We won't see it workin' which is too bad. We'll leave him a note, so he knows we need some flour."

As we rounded the corner to the front of the building, I couldn't help but make an audible gasp, "Oh my!"

This looked like a picture from an expensive magazine or calendar - an ancient old stone building covered in moss with an old wheel sitting in a sluice attached to the building. The building appeared to be shuttered up. On the front door was a chalk board and a piece of chalk on a string.

Shavon went up to the chalk board and wrote, "20 kg of flour – Shavon will pick up Friday a.m."

Excitedly I spoke, "When we come back will…?" I paused, searching my memory banks for the owner's name Shavon had just told me.

Sharon filled in my blank with, "Liam."

I continued, "When we come back will Liam allow me to take a picture of this? This is absolutely breath taking! I must send this picture to my mother. She would love it!"

Shavon grinned and replied, "Liam would love that. He's always willin' to share the beauty of the mill. He also loves givin' tours."

Alchemy of the Heart: Shavon Sun Cloud

I walked around the mill two additional times with my mouth open in awe. I don't think I had before ever seen a building this beautiful, this old, and this functioning.

Once I had finished admiring the building I walked back over and stood beside Shavon. I grinned and excitedly asked, "What's next?"

Shavon grinned at my boyish, impish excitement. She asked, "Ow about we go back to the cottage and have lunch?"

In typical Devin fashion, I shrugged my shoulders and replied, "OK. "

With that agreement between us, we turned and followed the route we had just taken to get here. We walked leisurely back to the cottage.

As we emerged from the woods into the open area that the cottage was magically centered in, I could not help but smile. This quaint and spectacular image of the cottage was beginning to etch itself deeply into my mind.

By the time we got done heating our simple lunch of unleavened bread with locally made butter, we were hungry. Maybe the better term would be ravenous. We both devoured our lunches!

After we cleaned up and put our lunch dishes away, Shavon explained where her car was parked and asked me to bring back to the cottage the two trunks that I had loaded into the boot yesterday.

Once I understood where the car was parked, I gladly wandered off to fulfill my apprentice role.

I knew the trunks were sacred, and I knew I had to be careful with them. I had forgotten how heavy they were. I had to stop a couple of times to gingerly put them down on the ground to give my body a rest. Sheesh, they were heavy!

Once both trunks were safely tucked into the cottage, I asked Shavon, "What's next?"

"Firewood for the firepit and for inside the cottage. We'll also need lots o' smaller wood to start our fires easily."

I spent the better part of the afternoon splitting wood and piling it in various locations. I piled wood inside the cottage, near the firepit, and also by a small firepit near the labyrinth.

When I came back from piling wood near the labyrinth, I saw Shavon put her mobile phone in her pocket. She told me, "Oi ordered more wood. Me friend Ciaran will drop off wood tomorrow beside me car. He'll leave us a cart to 'aul the wood to the woodshed. Once we're done with the cart, we'll leave it beside the car, and he'll pick it up from there."

Alchemy of the Heart: Shavon Sun Cloud

I shrugged, "Okay, but I suspect there is no 'we' in this hauling wood. The 'we' is just little ole' Devin."

Shavon flashed a playful grin, "Ye catch on fast." She paused and playfully asked, "Devin, would ye be a dear and put the kettle on for some tea? Oi'm goin' to change into me togs."

I abruptly stopped. "Togs?" I asked inquisitively.

Shavon grinned, "Togs. Swimsuit to those who're uncivilized or uncultured 'eathens."

I chuckled, "Evidently, I am not civilized nor cultured as I have never heard the term togs."

Shavon grinned as she moved towards the cottage, "Apparently." With that, she calmly opened the door, and entered the cottage, closing the door behind her. This effectively ended all conversation.

I could do nothing more than go get the kettle off the table near the firepit and wander over to the pump.

Once I had filled the kettle and placed it over top of the firepit, I wandered over to the outdoor cupboard and got two mugs and the teapot.

Shavon came out bare legged, with some sort of wrap around her bottom half. She was wearing a green bikini top. If I hadn't seen a glimpse of her figure these past few days, I would have been in big trouble. I would have been caught staring open-mouthed at her. Her figure was stunning!

I was trying really hard to remind myself that she was my teacher and friend and not some lustful image for me to drool over. I was trying, but her pure beauty made it difficult.

I would give Shavon credit - if she noticed me more than just looking, she didn't say a thing. She simply commented, "Oh good, you got the mugs."

It was then I noticed she was carrying her guitar as well.

As the tea was properly steeping, I went in and put on my swimsuit. Once I was changed, we took our tea to the swimming hole.

At the creek Shavon instructed me to pull out some lumber that was stacked nearby. She directed me how to build a couple of simple long benches for us to sit on.

Once the bench construction was done, we each sat down on our own bench and enjoyed our tea in silence for a few moments, blissfully enjoying the scenery. It was good to take a few moments to simply enjoy the day.

After a beautifully long, peaceful break, Shavon casually leaned over and handed me a couple of sheets of paper. She commented,

Alchemy of the Heart: Shavon Sun Cloud

"These are the lyrics o' couple songs we're goin' to sin' this weekend."

I squeaked out, "We?"

Shavon smiled, "Yes, we. Ye 'ave a great voice, Devin. Oi'm goin' to ask ye to sing 'armony with me. I would like us to practise a few times before the workshop.

Oi've some traditional Celtic songs, a few songs from the Shipibo tribe in Peru, and then three English songs that ye'll sin' with me. They're straightforward songs: All is Welcome Here; Butterfly People; and People of Love."

She further instructed, "Oi'll sing the song first and ye join in the next round."

All I could do was shrug my shoulders and respond, "Okay!"

Shavon teasingly laughed, "Yahr goin' to 'ave to find a more dignified way to respond!"

I grinned and bowed, "Yes m' lady."

Shavon squealed, "Oh! Oi love this version much better, m' lord!" We both laughed out loud at our frivolity.

After Shavon quit giggling over our shared humour, she reached over and picked up her guitar. She strummed it a few times to

Alchemy of the Heart: Shavon Sun Cloud

ensure it was still in tune before starting to sing the song 'All is welcome here.'

As the time came closer for me to join in, visions of my youth flooded back into my consciousness. I was instantly transported back in time - I was once again a little boy in grade school fearfully reciting a poem in front of the whole school.

As I tentatively sung the first few words of 'All is Welcome Here', I could feel my right leg began to shake ever so slightly, as if I was seven years old again.

Shavon must have noticed the pitchiness in my voice. Without missing a beat or messing up the lyrics to the song she was beautifully singing, she added in, "Ground, Devin, ground. Feel the connection to the earth."

I couldn't help but notice that when I was able to ground myself, my voice was less pitchy. When I slipped back into in my head, remembering all the terrors of growing up, my voice was a train wreck.

Even though it was only the two of us, it took me a long time to be comfortable singing loudly without liquid courage (beer) coursing through my veins.

Shavon stopped playing and set down her guitar but continued to sing. While still singing she took off her wrap.

Alchemy of the Heart: Shavon Sun Cloud

If I wasn't already distracted by my fears of singing and reliving the hardships of my youth, I was further distracted by seeing Shavon in her bikini! My gosh, she had an incredible figure!

Shavon walked over to me and said, "Take 'old of me 'and."

It wasn't so much a request as it was a gentle, yet firm command. I was still struggling to sing properly as I took hold of her hand. Then, like some ancient magical spell was cast over me, the very second I touched Shavon's hand my voice dropped into a beautiful harmonic, fully synchronized with her voice. My body relaxed, and my leg instantly stopped shaking.

While continuing to hold my hand Shavon led me to the creek, still joyfully singing all the way. Once my legs touched the cool water, I slowly felt my tactile senses begin to heighten and I stopped being so much in my head. I could feel the difference within me when I focused on the sensations of the water on my body. I could no longer hold onto all the self-deprecating conversations in my head. I was unable to bring up all those fearful memories. If a memory did pop up, the sensation of the cool water minimized the feelings.

Without straining our voices, we spent our time quietly singing, playing, and swimming in the creek. This helped me to stay grounded and concentrate on the lyrics of the songs rather than Shavon's fabulous figure. Even through my terrified and flighty mental state, I had stayed keenly aware of how striking Shavon was in her green bikini.

We sang and held hands on our way back to the cottage from the creek, too. Once we arrived at the cottage, I was instructed to drink the warm lemon water, which Shavon seemed to have made appear out of thin air. I certainly didn't remember her making the concoction, which was soothing to my throat as we prepared supper.

Supper was a casual affair of unleavened bread, the last of the stew and a surprise – a delicious apple pie, which we heated in a cast iron pot over the firepit. The pie was perfect – a nice golden brown. It was an awesome finishing touch to the day.

Shavon told me she uses this pot to bake foods all the time. It was horribly humbling to know that if there were ever any zombie apocalypse, I would not be able to survive long. I would starve to death without prepared meals. I lacked the knowledge and skills to cook things from scratch.

Shavon asked me not to talk too much that evening to help save my voice. Since we didn't talk much, we both headed to bed early.

The next morning, we were up early and Shavon asked, as she was brushing her hair, "Ye up for a long walk for breakfast?"

Alchemy of the Heart: Shavon Sun Cloud

Just as I started to shrug, I couldn't help but chuckle out loud, and shifted my shoulder shrug to a bow. I laughingly replied, "Of course, m' lady."

Shavon gleefully giggled and offered me a curtsey, "Oh, much better, m' lord. Oi love this!"

As we exited the cottage together to go for breakfast, Shavon started to sing,

"We are the people,
The people of love
Let us people love today.
We are the people,
The people of love
Let us people love today.

We are one
Under the sun
Let your heart sing it this way
Love is something
As free as the wind
I give it to you
And I'll give it again.

We are the people,
The people of love
Let us people love today.

Alchemy of the Heart: Shavon Sun Cloud

We are the people,
The people of love
Let us people love today.

Reach out to
The one you don't know
And give him
A helping hand
The time has come
For a sacrifice
To find the way
To our love.

We are the people,
The people of love
Let us people love today.

Love today, love today, love today, love today.

We are the people,
The people of love
Let us people love today.
We are the people,
The people of love
Let us people love today.

Alchemy of the Heart: Shavon Sun Cloud

Love today, love today, love today, love today,
Love today, love today, love today, love today.[2]

We sang as we passed by her car and happily continued singing as we walked down the road, heading somewhere for breakfast. I knew not where I was and had no idea where we were going.

We sang and talked for what appeared to be an hour. Then all of a sudden, we appeared in a tiny little village with a pub. Typical Oireland. Every little village has a pub.

Like every little pub we entered, Shavon was treated like a special guest, and everyone knew her. The robust owner welcomed her, "Ow are ye doin' Shavahn?"

In a mere instant, Shavon's Irish lilt got thicker as she spoke to the owner, "Oi'm doin' well. Oi'm up at mahm's cahttage fahr a weekend wahrkshop. Dis is me friend, Devahn."

Faster than a frog's tongue chasing a fly, I was enveloped in a massive friendly hug, "Good to meet ye, Devahn. Any friend o' Shavahn is a friend o' mine."

We were interrupted many times throughout our breakfast as the locals kept coming over to say, "Ello." Many of them came over just to get a look at me; they asked in various ways, "Is dis de boy ye fancy?"

---

[2] 'People of Love', song by Snatum Kaur

Alchemy of the Heart: Shavon Sun Cloud

Shavon responded with a playful yet firm, "Oi fancy dis boy. But 'e's 'ere to learn de ways o' de craft." This generally stopped the inquisition, "What ye doin' wid a yank?"

When we were done breakfast, Shavon ordered and paid for several individual-sized Shepard pies and a couple of veggie pies for us. Apparently, this would be supper on Friday night for everyone in the workshop.

I still didn't know what we were doing in this workshop, but at least I knew what we were having for supper Friday night. If I had been more observant, I would have paid attention to the number of pies Shavon ordered so that I would know how many participants to expect.

As we walked back to the cottage, Shavon made sure I knew the way back to the pub. Apparently, I was now the official Uber Eats© delivery mechanism.

Part of the way back Shavon said, "Let's 'ave some fun. Close yahr eyes as we walk back to the cottage. Keep yahr eyes closed for as long as ye can."

With that, Shavon closed her eyes and continued to walk as if she could see the road completely. Tentatively I closed my eyes and began walking the road. I sensed that I was walking like a drunkard, staggering from edge to edge of the road. I was barely better than a dunk on a Saturday night staggering home.

Alchemy of the Heart: Shavon Sun Cloud

We walked with our eyes closed for a relatively long time. I was slower than Shavon. When I could no longer hear her light footsteps on the packed soil, I dutifully carried on without opening my eyes.

Suddenly, ever so quietly, this nagging little voice in my head said, "Turn right, Devin." It was the same voice that told me to duck just before I hit the tree branch back at the farm. I hesitated in my tracks.

My overly active mind wondered, "Do I go forward or right?"

Then I remembered that Shavon trusted her gut big time. She even delivered a package to the same hospital I was at, which led her to find me. "Look how that turned out, Devin," I thought. "Just because she trusted the little voice in her head."

I shuffled to my right and began to move again, ever so slowly. Over my left shoulder, I heard clapping. Then I heard Shavon's voice, "Very good, Devin. Yahr intuition served ye well."

I opened my eyes just a little bit and looked to my left to see Shavon leaning against her car. She had a huge smile on her face. "Very well, very well," were her words of encouragement.

She stopped leaning on the car, stood upright and moved towards me. "Lesson is over, Devin. Let's go to the cottage."

Alchemy of the Heart: Shavon Sun Cloud

I opened my eyes fully, nodded, and replied, "Yes, m' lady!" We both laughed and headed back to the cottage.

No sooner had we arrived back at the cottage when we heard the distinctive sounds of a lory being backed up, followed up by loud clattering. I had to assume that was the sound of blocks of wood being dumped off the truck. I grinned, "I guess I know what I am doing this morning."

Shavon smirked, "Apparently so."

As I turned to go to the newly dumped wood pile, Shavon said, "Oi'll put the kettle on for tea."

I cheerfully responded, "Thank you, m' lady."

I spent the better part of the morning filling up a four wheeled cart and hauling wood from the parking lot to the wood pile. Shavon gave me very specific instructions on how and where to pile the wood. She even came out a few times to check on my progress and the quality of my stacking job.

After I stacked the last log onto the pile, I took a couple of steps back and proudly thought to myself, "Not bad, not bad at all."

I absent-mindedly turned to go find Shavon and almost leapt out of my skin. She was mere inches away! I hadn't heard her sneak up behind me. I let out a startled, "Nahhh!" and stumbled back in surprise. Apparently, I was no meerkat; meerkats are always on guard and aware.

"Are ye all right?"

"Yes, but you sure scared the heck out of me!" I stammered, "It seems I was concentrating a little hard."

Shavon grinned, "Apparently so. Oi came to tell you lunch is ready."

Lunch was soup, salad and, once again, unleavened fried bread. The bread was super tasty.

An idea abruptly popped into my little hamster wheel of a brain out of nowhere. I looked over at Shavon and waited for her to take a bite of her food before I asked her, "I have noticed we are drinking herbal tea and enjoying unleavened bread that I assume is made of whole wheat flour. I am also assuming the bread has no sugar. Our meals, as usual, are all vegetarian, but rather..." I paused, searching my brain for the correct word, "Healthier than the already healthy version of our earlier meals! Is this on purpose?"

Shavon grinned and nodded her head in acknowledgement. She began chewing her food furiously so she could swallow and answer my question. I couldn't help but smile at my childish prank to get back at her.

Alchemy of the Heart: Shavon Sun Cloud

Once Shavon had completely chewed her food and taken a sip of her tea, she replied, "It is," and then took another bite of bread.

I couldn't help but laugh, "Touche! It seems two can play this game."

Shavon vigorously nodded her head in agreement. I made a mental note. I could wait her out. So, I got up, took the kettle off the firepit, and walked over to the well. I filled the kettle and placed it back onto the hook to let the water boil.

I returned to my seat, picked up my warm tea, and took a sip. Shavon almost choked on her food. Judging from the wicked grin on her face, she just figured out that a game was now afoot. I could visibly see her slow down her eating. She was intentionally chewing her food very, very... very slowly!

I smiled and stood back up. "Excuse me m' lady!"

I sauntered over to the cottage where I grabbed my soap, a towel, and a clean t-shirt. When I stepped back outside Shavon looked at me inquisitively and asked, "What ye goin' to do now?"

I smirked, "First, I am going to pile all the dishes near the outdoor sinks. Then I'm going to the swimming hole to wash my sweat off. After that, I will come back and do the dishes."

Shavon laughed, "Oh, yahr good, Devin, very good. We're eatin' 'ealthier because o' de ceremonies we're goin' to do. Oi want people to eat 'ealthy for a few days before the ceremonies. It's better for everyone if we 'aven't eaten processed food prior to the weekend."

She paused and playfully added, "We can't expect people to eat 'ealthy if we don't set a great example, now, can we?"

I grinned, "Yes, m' lady, we need to lead by example."

With a more serious expression on my face, I asked, "I am off to the swimming hole. Are you coming?"

Shavon cocked her head and abruptly stood up, "Of course! Oi'll be just a moment. Don't leave without me." She bounded into the cottage.

Shavon returned a short while later with a small wicker basket full of what appeared to be beauty products and a couple of towels. Without stopping or waiting for me, she headed directly towards the creek and began to sing, "*Broken hearts, broken wings. Bring it all, everything. Bring the song you fear to sing. All is welcome here...*"[3]

We sang in harmony all the way to the creek. Then things got a little uncomfortable for me.

As I was carefully setting down the shirt I had pulled over my head, I noticed Shavon had removed her cover up, revealing her

---

[3] 'All is Welcome Here', song by Deva Premal & Miten

beautiful green bikini top. She was reaching behind her back in what I could only assume was a move to remove her top. In an automatic male response, I think my jaw hit the ground and my bottom lip started dragging in the sand. My inner neanderthal roared in a confused and bewildered panic, forcing me to ask, "What are you doing??"

Shavon paused and chuckled slightly, "Oh, Oi forgot, yahr from America."

She stopped what she was doing. Her facial expression became serious yet remained soft and caring. "Devin, as we learn to let go o' personal baggage and uncover our inner truths, we're effectively stripping away everything in our lives so we can be reborn, figuratively and literally, into the person we've always wanted to become. One o' de ways is through de-sexualization of the human body and learning to totally accept yahr own body.

Many, but not all o' de modern faiths have sexualized the human body as a means o' controlling the followers of the faith. The ancient teachings from many different cultures, on the other 'and, provide us with an opportunity to appreciate the human form without sexualizing it.

As we move into and deepen your lessons, Devin, yahr goin' to have to get comfortable with the human form without clothes on. That means yours and another's…includin' mine."

Alchemy of the Heart: Shavon Sun Cloud

Shavon gently locked eyes with me, sussing me out, "Devin, do ye think this is goin' to be an issue?"

Uncomfortably I shifted weight from one foot to the other. My face turned redder and redder, "You remember the talk we had a while ago where we agreed we would be truthful to each other?"

Shavon nodded her head in agreement.

My ears turned crimson red. My head could be mistaken for a bright red balloon. I began stammering, "Well you know, you know how we Americans stand at attention when we hear our anthem? It is just what we do."

Shavon replied with a drawn out suspicious, "Aaaaand?"

The words that came out of my mouth next were almost a whisper. It was like I was reluctantly offering top-secret, highly classified information. Truthfully, turning over state secrets seemed to be an easier thing to do than telling Shavon what I was about to share. "I have never had a girlfriend, never been with anyone. So, I am thinking that seeing a naked body could be the equivalent to hearing a national anthem for me. Certain body parts will just naturally want to stand up at attention." As those words escaped my lips, my whole body flushed to an incredible crimson tone.

Shavon didn't laugh, smirk, or make me feel like less of a man for admitting one of my deepest-held secrets. Instead, she walked over to me with a tender smile on her face. She stopped and stood directly in front of me. With her right hand, she gently touched my cheek. "Devin, one o' de things Oi truly love about ye is yahr willin'ness to be authentic and share what's goin' on with ye no matter how embarrassin' ye perceive yahr share to be."

She continued, "If Oi've one ask of ye, it's that ye never lose that trait." Shavon grinned a very sly grin, "Okay, Oi've two asks - that ye don't lose yahr willingness to share and that ye trust me. Together we'll deal with..." Shavon's grin turned devilishly wicked, "Together we'll deal with whatever comes up," emphasizing the word 'up'.

I didn't think it was possible for my face and body to turn a deeper crimson red, but after Shavon uttered the word 'up' I flushed an even deeper shade of red... red, red!

I held Shavon's gaze with a deep sense of trepidation and a faint glimmer of willingness to trust her. In spite of dreading the million deaths I would die if my body didn't behave properly, I squeaked, "Okay."

Shavon leaned over and kissed me on the cheek. "Thank ye for the trust." Then she turned and walked back to where her towel, soaps and lotions were sitting. With no ceremony nor a second thought of the demon she could release in her terrified student behind her, she slipped off her top and walked into the creek.

Alchemy of the Heart: Shavon Sun Cloud

I fearfully looked to the sky; no ominous clouds were forming. I was relieved that my immediate thought of getting struck down by lightning wasn't going to occur. Without looking down, I knew my biggest fear wasn't happening either. So, I slipped off my swimming trunks and joined Shavon in the creek.

Sometime in between washing our hair and swimming, Shavon went ashore and removed her bottoms. I was still keenly aware of how beautiful she was and that she indeed had an incredible figure, but somehow, I was able to keep a sense of proper decorum.

Once we were washed and dried, we slowly headed back to the cottage. We didn't even bother putting on clothes. We sang all the way back and this time it was me that started singing first, *"Broken hearts, broken wings. Bring it all, everything Bring the song you fear to sing. All is welcome here..."* The singing helped take my mind off the fact that I was naked with a beautiful woman, and I was not burning in hell...yet! There was always tomorrow.

When we arrived back at the cottage, Shavon said, "Tonight we'll drink mushroom tea again. This time a smaller dose for ye."

I nodded my head and replied in a very drawn-out, theatrical tone, "Yes, m' lady."

Shavon chuckled, "Oi love it."

I turned and faced the firepit. I prudently thought, "Clothes would be a good thing if I am going to play around the fire. I got burned once with fire; I don't need a second experience." I went into the cottage and put on my ceremonial clothes.

When I exited the cottage with my ceremonial clothes on Shavon looked at me with that look of, "Well done, Devin."

I explained, "I am leery of the fire. I didn't want you to have to nurse me back to health from burns for the second time! I knew we were doing a ceremony, so I thought I should dress for the occasion."

Shavon beamed. "Great call." With that, she headed into the cottage.

I began to build up the fire. I carefully set the kettle on the hook that never moved from the firepit. Quietly I began to sing to help me remember the lyrics for the upcoming retreat.

When Shavon reappeared at the fire in her full ceremony regalia, she was holding a few apples, a little bit of left-over unleavened bread, and a couple of different sliced-up cheeses.

When I questioned the addition of a Guiness™ to our supper, Shavon's defense was boisterous, "There's no artificial flavours or ingredients in the beer!"

Once the dishes were washed up and put away, we went into the cottage to build our private little nests. In my mind, I wondered,

Alchemy of the Heart: Shavon Sun Cloud

"What bird or animal builds a nest with therm-a-rest pads and piles and piles of blankets?"

Learning from my first adventure with the tea, I decided I wouldn't use as many blankets in my nest; it was just too darn hot. Nonetheless, I set a few extra blankets close by, just in case my second experience differed from my first.

Once our nests were set up, we headed back outside to make the tea. I wandered off to retrieve the mugs and honey from the cupboard. Typically, I would have served m' lady tea in a proper teacup, but I was told that for ceremonies we use mugs in case we drop our cups. Shavon had said, "Mugs are more likely to survive, and they 'old more."

After I dropped the mugs and honey off, I inquired, "Where's the ginger stored?"

Shavon sheepishly laughed out loud, "Sorry about that. Oi thought Oi showed ye where everythin' was. Apparently, Oi didn't take ye on the whole tour."

Shavon stopped pulverizing the mushrooms, wiped her hands on the cloth sitting on the table, and waved to me, "Follow me."

I followed her around the back of the cottage to the cupboard I had just been at and she opened the bottom right door. There was a big drawer that leaned out at a 45-degree angle and two medium-sized drawers that pulled out. Shavon said, "The large one is for the potatoes. The two medium drawers are for carrots and onions." She opened each drawer for me to inspect and indeed there were small amounts of each veggie in the drawers.

Playfully, a grin of astonishment washed over my face. I retorted, "That's amazing!"

Shavon laughed and playfully responded, "Oi know."

Shavon opened the lower door and behind that were shelves of sealed containers labelled flour, baking powder, and baking soda. There were also some smaller drawers similar to those I had already inspected. Shavon opened each one. One had garlic, one had ginger, and another held numerous salt and pepper shakers.

Shavon carefully closed each of the drawers and the cupboard doors. She gazed at me, "It's a good thing ye asked, Devin! Now ye know where almost everythin' is. Ye'll be our quartermaster for the weekend. Ye'll be the one to show our participants where everythin' is.

This retreat 'as us preparin' meals as a community. Friday night we'll 'ave prepared meat and veggie pies, but for the rest of the weekend meals we'll prepare some variation of stew, bread and cheese, closer to a traditional Oirish meal from our past."

Shavon waved me to follow her, "Let's go back and finish our tea."

Alchemy of the Heart: Shavon Sun Cloud

I followed her around to the front of the cottage and retrieved the now-boiled water from the kettle off the fire. I was about to prepare my tea when Shavon cursed out loud, "Drat!"

I was mildly startled, "What did we forget now?"

Shavon chuckled, "There is no we in this. It was all me, but thanks for bein' willin' to share the blame!"

Then Shavon spoke in that tone that indicated it was time for me to shut up and be the student... again.

"Last night we 'onoured yahr North American ancestry and used a common version of the First Peoples' four directions. Today we're goin' to use the Celtic Cup o' Truth. In times gone by the Celtic Cup o' Truth was mentioned in Celtic lore and is repeated in 'istorical storytellin'.

We see it first referenced in lore as the magic cup belongin' to Manannan Mac Lir who passed it on to Cormac Mac Airt, a mythical high king of Oireland and one o' de most celebrated kings in Oirish tradition. He was sometimes given the epithet Ulfhada (longbearded), which denoted his great wisdom. He was portrayed as an ideal king whose power brought good fortune and prosperity to the whole country.

Legends of the cup vary, including one in which the cup detects truth from lies o' de one drinking from the cup. There are also references to the cup being the holy grail in Arthurian supposition.

Alchemy of the Heart: Shavon Sun Cloud

Whatever the origin o' de cup, each person in the linage Oi follow - and that you now walk behind - is given a quest to find a cup. The only instructions given are as follows: it must be found in yahr travels; it must be gifted to ye; and lastly, ye'll know this is yahr cup of truth when yahr in possession of it. Since ye'll drink from it, Oi suggest it not be lead or pewter." Shavon grinned and continued, "Nothin' like yahr Cup o' Truth makin' you sick!"

Shavon's face morphed into a serious matronly expression, "Devin, as a man and a student of mine, do ye agree to undertake the quest for a Cup o' Truth? Knowin', like the branch ye walked into on yahr first real day of training, the Cup o' Truth may sting slightly?"

She paused and asked, "Do ye willin'ly and openly take on the quest? Even though it may take years to find the right cup?"

When Shavon uttered the last syllable of her invitation to take on this quest, it was like my body was in a Star Trek episode. I was instantly transported back to the Middle Ages where I was nobility once again. I knew to the very core of my being that my word was my law.

It was kind of weird. I felt grounded and completely sincere as I spoke the words, "I understand, and I freely take on the quest of finding my Cup of Truth."

Alchemy of the Heart: Shavon Sun Cloud

Shavon smiled and nodded her head in acknowledgement, "So it is."

After a pause, she continued, "In the meantime, Devin, select a mug from all these mugs and 'onour it as yahr Cup o' Truth until a new mug appears for ye. Select one that feels right for ye."

Shavon slowly stepped back. A quiet calm fell upon the kitchen area as I looked over the assortment of mugs. I have no idea why, but I closed my eyes and let my hands hover over the mugs for a few moments. Then, like a magnet drawn to iron, my right hand was inexplicitly pulled over to a mug. When I had a secure hold of the mug, a tingly sensation coursed through my arm. This was followed by a deep sense of "This is absolutely the right mug!" that filled my body completely. I opened my eyes.

The mug was a plain mug that was painted two shades of red. To my overactive imagination, it appeared that the mug was painted a light red and then a second coat of darker, blood red was allowed to drip down the sides. It was like blood overflowing from the center of the mug, dripping down the sides.

Shavon raised her eyebrow with an inquisitive look. "An interesting selection, Mr. Jones."

I could only shrug my shoulders. "It was what called to me, m' lady!"

With that Shavon waved, "Follow me m' lord, if ye would."

Alchemy of the Heart: Shavon Sun Cloud

I nodded my head, "Of course m' lady!"

We headed into the cottage, and she went straight to her bed. She bent down and slid out an aged trunk. Carefully, with reverence for her precious cargo, she untied the ribbon that acted as a lock for the weathered trunk. Gently lifting the lid, she took out a small satchel. Purposefully, she untied the satchel and gingerly removed a small pottery cup. The cup had no handle on it. To my untrained, novice eyes it looked like a small pot and not a cup, but who was I to question whether it was a cup or pot? Shavon gingerly put the now-empty satchel back in the trunk, carefully closed the lid, and slid the trunk back under the bed.

Shavon turned and faced me. Truth is, it was almost a twirl, like a little girl showing off a prized possession. She held up the cup and shared, "Oi got this cup when Oi was in Kenya. A Maasai woman gave me the cup. Her name was Naserian, which means 'peaceful one'.

Oi lived in Kenya with the Maasai people and Naserian for six months learnin' about their culture. This cup was one o' Naserian's mother's cups. Naipanoi was her mother's name which means 'hard working'. Naipanoi made this cup when she was very young. Naipanoi was a gifted potter who eventually sold pottery to tourists to support her family. When Oi left Kenya, her pottery was still in demand, many years after her death."

Alchemy of the Heart: Shavon Sun Cloud

I was amazed and told her so. "Shavon, you are amazing. You have travelled so much. I never thought about travelling until I met you. I would probably still be at my dead-end job if I had not met you!"

Shavon added, "Ye mean if ye'd not burned your feet."

I guffawed, "Okay, rub it in some more! Yes, if I had not burned my feet." I added extra emphasis on the word burned.

Shavon protested, "Devin, Oi'm not rubbing it in. Oi mean if ye'd completed the fire walk, ye could have taken a completely different path in yahr life. Devin, ye'd 'ave completely distinct new lessons and teachers in yahr life. If the universe wanted us to meet, maybe ye would have been that annoying American tourist Oi met somewhere on a flight, and we'd never 'ave the opportunity to really get to know each other."

It was my turn to chuckle, "I would also not have met the very wise and scholarly fish."

Shavon laughed, "Correct!"

After a few more heartfelt chuckles she continued with her lesson, "It was all perfect in its timin'. We may not like the timin' o' our lessons or be comfortable with them, but when we look back at our life, we're able to see 'ow our misfortunes are some of our most profound gifts."

Alchemy of the Heart: Shavon Sun Cloud

I had to nod my head in agreement because I knew in my heart, she was right.

Shavon smiled and started to walk towards the door, "Let's go make our tea." She stopped abruptly and looked at me with a serious expression, "Devin, be open to findin' yahr Cup o' Truth at any time. The cup or mug or container will show at the darndest time and may be o' de most unexpected shape. As ye may have already judged, me Cup o' Truth looks a lot like a mini plant pot. But it is me Cup o' Truth.

Each person has their own story behind their cup. One of me students, Amelia, has a very old copper cup that her great, great grandfather kept his pencils in. He was a cartographer in the 1800's when drawin' maps was a true craft. When she was a child, her grandfather told her stories o' her great, great grandfathers' explorations. Amelia – ye'll meet her this weekend - knew she wanted the cup, but she didn't know why until she became me student. Her quest to find her cup lasted only a couple of days. She 'ad to travel to her mother's 'ome to get the cup.

On the other 'and, Lucy's quest lasted almost ten years. She was drinkin' from a China teacup aboard a luxury cruise ship off the coast of Antarctica. It suddenly struck her that she'd traveled to every continent in the world. She realized she'd done somethin' not many people in the world 'ad done before. In her mind, she was part of the 1%. Holdin' that teacup on that cruise ship signified to her that she'd made it and was worthy of all her dreams. Needless to say, Lucy kept the teacup and it's been her Cup o' Truth ever since.

Devin, ye'll know when yahr Cup o' Truth appears before ye."

Lesson completed, she turned toward the door and headed out. I knew to follow her, so I scooted out the door, too.

I went to the firepit and checked on the water. It was off the boil, so I removed the kettle from the hook and stoked up the fire. I hung the kettle again so the water would come back to a boil. After that, I went to the cupboard to collect the ginger, honey, and a couple of spoons.

I returned from the storage cupboard to find Shavon lifting the kettle off the fire and grinning at me, "Thanks for all the work yahr doin'. It 'elps a lot. It'll be fantastic to 'ave you 'ere this weekend for three reasons: one – for all the 'elp ye'll be, and two - for the masculine energy ye bring, and three - to 'elp with the swimmers." She grinned, "Yahr not the only one that goes swimmin' because o' the tea."

In a mockingly defensive tone, I squeaked out, "You strip off your clothes and run naked into a stream once, and you are forever labelled as a swimmer."

Shavon nodded her head while an impish grin spread like a rash across her face, "True."

Alchemy of the Heart: Shavon Sun Cloud

Once our tea was prepared and poured into our respective Cups of Truth, we took our cups into the cottage. Shavon looked about the room and declared, "Let's move our nests to the west side near the bed and look towards the door."

A few moments later we were comfortably sitting cross-legged in our nests facing the door with a great view of the fivefold symbol on the floor.

Shavon's voice once again shifted to her teacher's tone, "Let's breathe a nice deep breath."

We both inhaled deeply. Shavon instructed, "Breathe in deeply again," which we both did.

To allow the sacredness of what we were doing to settle in, Shavon paused for a few moments before she spoke, "Let's raise our cups to de direction o' east and de element o' air to 'onour our own personal truth."

I watched as she raised her cup in the air, solemnly said, "To truth" then brought her cup to her lips and took a small sip.

Shavon waited a moment before she spoke, "Let's raise our cups to de direction o' south and de element o' fire and 'onour what we know to be universal truth."

Again, she raised her cup in the air, said, "To truth" then brought her cup to her lips and took a small sip.

Alchemy of the Heart: Shavon Sun Cloud

This time I mimicked her actions and said, "To truth" before I took a sip, too.

Shavon once again paused for a moment before she spoke, "Let's raise our cups to de direction o' west and de element o' water and 'onour what we know to be absolute truth." She raised her cup in the air, said, "To truth" then brought her cup to her lips and took a small sip."

Once again, I mimicked her actions and words.

I couldn't help but smile. I was slowly beginning to understand the process of the ceremony. Yes, sometimes I am not the sharpest knife in the drawer, but eventually, I do catch on.

This time I knew Shavon was going to pause for a moment before she spoke, "Let's raise our cups to de direction o' north and de element of earth and 'onour what we believe to be objective truth."

This time I was able to follow along with her, as we raised our glasses and said, "To truth," before taking a sip.

On the final round, Shavon spoke, ""Let's raise our cups to de location o' center within us, de universe, and de element o' spirit and 'onour what we know to be de elixir of forgiveness, de cup of knowledge."

Once again, we raised our cups in the air and solemnly said, "To truth", then brought our cups to our lips and took a small sip.

Alchemy of the Heart: Shavon Sun Cloud

We both fell silent, each of us lost in our own musing while gazing at the five-fold symbol on the floor.

As I took the last few remaining sips of my now slightly warm elixir, I realized that for the next ceremony, I needed to take smaller sips so I wouldn't drink all the tea by the end of the ceremony.

I sat my cup down on the floor. I also realized that for the next ceremony I needed to bring my water bottle. My lips were a little parched and I could use some water to wet them.

I leaned back and carefully dug myself into the safety of my little nest, leaving only my face uncovered. In my mind, I looked like a baby Kangaroo peering out of the safety of its mother's pouch. I couldn't help but snort at the thought of me as a little Joey, safely tucked away in a giant kangaroo pouch.

Like a mosquito off in the distance gradually getting closer and becoming louder, I started to hear the music from a 70's song that I vaguely knew. It was Pink Floyd's song, "Time". As the music intensified, so did the temperature of my face. I could feel beads of sweat rolling down my forehead. Then colored, spinning, geometric, intertwined gears began to slowly appear in my vision. The colors intensified until the sensation of music and colors was incredibly hypnotic. The gears were turning in multiple directions and dimensions at the same time, crossing and fading into each other, pulsating, and moving to the tempo of the music. My consciousness became lost as it merged into the musical sensation.

With each passing moment, my body's energy dissipated. First, my arms felt weak, and then my legs… I was slowly getting weaker and weaker with each measured ticking of time with each rhythmic beat of the song.

Then, in my magic mushroom-induced state, my body began to merge into the earth! I was totally engrossed with becoming the soil itself.

Then in a blinding flash, I was floating outside of my body. I watched with morbid fascination as the ants and worms systematically disposed of my decomposing body. I was returning to earth as worm casings and ant poop!

This led my drug-enhanced, hyperactive mind to ponder, "Is this the meaning of life? Is life just POOP? Is that all there is to life - that we are all just poop in the end? Is life just one giant pile of poop?"

With the change in the beat of the music that was still playing in my mind, the thought "No!" flashed across my mind, quickly followed by the lyrics of the song, "People of Love" by Snatam Kaur:

Alchemy of the Heart: Shavon Sun Cloud

"We are the people
The people of love
Let us people love today…" [4]

In the very next moment, a giant starburst exploded inside my head. I was blinded by the sheer intensity of the light. It was like a giant flare went off under my eyelids. The vision of me dissolving into the earth was abruptly ripped from my brain and replaced with the sensation of my body being slowly covered in warm goo as I was unhurriedly filled with a rapturous sense of love - love that was beyond me, that included me, but was bigger and more expansive than anything I had ever experienced in my whole life. It was like my whole world was covered in a giant, warm, sticky, oozing, warm honey bath.

Slowly, like the sun going down after a wonderful day on the beach, I became engulfed in the realization that life was about love, about living life completely from a place of love. Living from the goodness of your heart no matter what was going on.

Holy SHIT! I finally understood why Shavon did what she did. I understood why she stayed those extra days to help a friend. Why she helped me at the hospital and why she paid for me to come to Ireland.

---

[4] 'People of Love', song by Snatum Kaur

Alchemy of the Heart: Shavon Sun Cloud

In a nanosecond, with a foothold in the present and in the ongoing eternity at the same time, I truly understood what unconditional love was. I absolutely understood at a cellular level what living a life of purposeful love was!

The word understanding couldn't accurately describe the knowing I was feeling. I knew that from this moment forward I carried this unconditional love at a cellular level. I knew what Shavon called an all-knowing truth.

This was the first of many truths to come.

I genuinely don't know how long I was lost in the space of awe at this 'understanding', but when I returned fully to the here and now, I was singing out loud, "We are the people, the people of love... Let us people love today!"

I could feel the blissful sensations of touch, smell, and sound gradually return to me in the present moment. Interestingly, it was the sensation of sound that arrived last.

Leisurely, and somewhat reluctantly, I opened my eyes. It took me a moment to find my bearings and bring the room into focus. Apparently, I was still slightly disoriented by my new experience of truth.

Systematically, I began searching the room for Shavon. When I finally found her, I saw that she was crying. It appeared her tears were not tears of terror or sorrow, but what I could best explain as tears of joy.

This explanation was a stretch for me, as I was not that experienced with the emotions of women, other than my mother. It was interesting to realize that I didn't know women very well. I had to smile, though, because if I was going to learn about women, I really lucked out having Shavon as my teacher and mentor.

As I continued to look at Shavon, I noticed her face was aglow. She was backlit by a shiny white light. I only knew the term backlit from watching a bunch of videos on how video creation is done.

In my partially drugged state, Shavon looked like one of the saints portrayed in the stained-glass windows in the many large churches I had attended throughout my life. This thought triggered me to wonder why we hadn't toured any of the cathedrals or churches while I was here in Ireland. I was going to have to ask Shavon about this in the near future.

Alchemy of the Heart: Shavon Sun Cloud

So it Begins... In Earnest

The next thing I remember is waking up in my cozy nest with a euphoric sensation of bliss. I peered over at Shavon and noted she was still asleep in the safety of her own nest.

Quietly and carefully, I unwrapped myself from the comfort of my warm nest. Ever so stealthily, I put on my shoes and exited the cottage, allowing Shavon to sleep a little longer. I suspected that throughout the upcoming weekend, she would be playing full-on. Her teaching persona would be very busy and have little time for rest. The least I could do was allow her the courtesy to sleep in.

I was off to make us some tea and see what I could create for breakfast. I had made a few meals at Shavon's house, but I wasn't in charge of anything while we were at the cottage.

Getting the fire relit in the morning was quite easy because the embers were still a little warm from the fire the night before, and the wood was dry.

Once the fire was lit and burning heartily, I filled the kettle at the well and placed it back on the hook over the firepit.

In perfect divine timing, my stomach growled, indicating that it was time to go to the cupboards and see what kind of food I could rustle up.

Alchemy of the Heart: Shavon Sun Cloud

I found eggs, green peppers, onions, broccoli, and a little spinach. With a little more digging and hunting around in the cupboard, I also found some unleavened bread. It was amazing what you could find when you went looking! Breakfast was going to be omelets with bread and tea.

As I was closing the cupboard doors, I was delighted to spy in the far reach of a corner a jar of raspberry jam. I grinned like I had won the lottery, which in turn made me chuckle out loud. The realization that I was getting excited over the simple pleasure of finding raspberry jam in a cupboard left me slightly amazed at myself. The old Devin would have never been excited about finding raspberry jam. He would have just said, "Yeah, OK!" But this new Devin, Devin version 2.0, was excited about finding raspberry jam in an outdoor cupboard at a cottage in the middle of nowhere in the middle of freaking Ireland. Now that was a cool thing to think about!

With a grin still on my face, I carried all the ingredients to the outdoor kitchen table using a cutting board as a tray. I was proud of myself for managing to bring everything in one trip.

I hesitated as I realized that I forgot to wash my hands. I simply shrugged and wandered over to the kettle to take the lukewarm water over to the wash basin. It felt good to wash my hands prior to playing with our food.

Alchemy of the Heart: Shavon Sun Cloud

I cut the vegetables into small pieces, looked around, and then groaned to myself. I did forget something. I forgot the huge cast iron pan. This pan was so different from any frying pan I had ever used at home. Instead of the typical straight handle that I was used to, it had a great big metal loop handle that slid over a hook on the firepit to keep it in place.

I wandered back to the cupboard and returned with the frying pan and oil – another thing I had forgotten on the first trip to the cupboard. Apparently, I didn't bring everything I needed!

I smiled at being able to do something for Shavon as I set the pan over the fire pit, then checked on the water in the kettle. The water was almost boiled.

I chuckled at my silliness as I headed back to the cupboard to get cups, the teapot, tea leaves, and honey. Apparently, Devin version 2.0 was as forgetful as Devin version 1.0!

I returned with all the tea fixings as well as plates, and a couple of knives to spread the jam with.

I took the water off the firepit and poured a little boiling water into the teapot to prewarm the teapot. Prior to coming to Ireland, I knew nothing about how to make a proper cup of tea.

Once the teapot was sufficiently warm, I swirled the water around and poured it out on the ground. Then I filled the teapot up with fresh hot water. I carefully measured the black tea leaves into the teapot, put the lid on, and dutifully noted the time on my watch. In six minutes, the tea would be ready.

I groaned out loud. I forgot a bowl to mix the eggs and vegetables in! I went back to the cupboard for the fourth time to get a clay bowl and a fork to mix with, as well as a spatula. "OK, I think that's finally everything I need!" I thought to myself.

By this time the frying pan was hot, and I could carefully add oil and the omelet mixture I had whipped up.

As I was tending to the omelets in the frying pan, I heard the cottage door open. Without turning around, I greeted Shavon, "Morning, sleepy head."

Shavon replied cheerfully, "Good mornin'. Wow! Yahr makin' breakfast."

I smiled as I looked at my watch, "You're welcome. Tea will be ready in one minute."

"Ye made tea as well? This is a blessed mornin'!"

Shavon moved towards the teapot and at the one-minute mark she poured two mugs of tea. She took a quick sip out of one cup and then brought the other one to me. With a small curtsey she held my cup out and offered. "Yahr tea m' lord."

I took the cup from her hands and graciously nodded my head in acknowledgement, "M' lady."

Alchemy of the Heart: Shavon Sun Cloud

I took a sip and handed her back the cup, "Thank you, m' lady, for the tea. Could I ask you to take this cup back to the table? I need to return my attention to the omelets. Breakfast will be ready shortly."

Shavon took my cup, offered another small curtsey and agreed, "Very good, m' lord."

As she set my cup on the table, Shavon spied water in the basin. She dipped her hands in the pan and squealed with delight, "M' lord, ye even warmed the water. How noble of ye!"

If I wasn't flipping the omelets, I would have bowed or nodded my head. The best I could do was respond enthusiastically, "You are most welcome, m' lady."

It seemed we were both rather hungry as we devoured our breakfasts quite quickly. When we were done, we quickly washed the dishes and cleaned up the kitchen area, leaving the grounds spotless.

We had just finished tidying up the cottage when our sacred silence was broken by the noise of a loud lory in the near distance. It sounded like it pulled up and parked in the area where Shavon's car was parked. I looked at Shavon with a rather perplexed look on my face, "Any guess who that is?"

Shavon shook her head, "Don't know, but let's go see."

Alchemy of the Heart: Shavon Sun Cloud

With that, we were headed down the path toward her car.

As we got closer, the noise level increased. We could also hear voices. Shavon smiled, "It's Liam and Daniel. They're doin' deliveries."

Shavon skipped a little as she picked up her pace. She rounded the path into the clearing where her car was parked and bellowed, "Ooze makin' all dis noise? 'Ave ye no respect fahr de sacredness o' dis land? De ruckus ye made could wake de dead!"

The taller of the two men stopped his unloading, headed towards Shavon, and countered with, "We wanted to give ye a chance to put yahr clahthes ahn. We 'ear yahr shacked up 'ere wit a yank."

Shavon retorted as she closed in on the men, "'E may be a yank, but 'e's more a gentleman dan ye two'll ever be!"

As Shavon and the rather handsome lad met, they stopped talking and genuinely embraced each other. They even exchanged a kiss on the lips, which surprised me. She kisses a lot of people on the cheeks, but none that I can remember on the lips! They held each other long enough for me to catch up and come stand beside Shavon.

As I came to a stop, the handsome lad broke free of his embrace with Shavon and quickly stuck out his right hand for a handshake. "'Ello. Me name is Liam. Pleased to meet ye! What's yahr name?"

Alchemy of the Heart: Shavon Sun Cloud

I couldn't help but be taken in by his enthusiasm and excitement. I enthusiastically returned his handshake, "My name is Devin. Pleased to meet you!"

While still shaking my hand he tipped his head towards the other lad, "De ahder blahke's name is Daniel. 'E owns de lahry. Oi just jumped in wit 'im tahday so ye wouldn't 'ave to carry de 20 kg o' flooehr frahm de mill to 'ere."

Shavon had moved over to affectionately hug Daniel. She said to him, "Let me guess. Ye two were gahssipin over a cooehple o' pints o' guiness last night and descahvered Oi was gettin' deliveries tahday."

It was Daniel's turn to speak, "Oi wouldn't say we were gahssipin. Rather we were tryin' to increase our delivery efficiencies and make sure our lettle sester was naht bein' taken advantage o' by de barbaric yank."

Liam let go of my hand and turned to face Shavon and Daniel. He nodded his head as he added, "We're just lookin' ooeht fahr our lettle sester."

I laughed out loud as I headed towards Daniel, "Ever think it was the Yank that needed looking after?" I asked him.

Shavon playfully slapped Daniel's shoulder, "'Ow lahng did it take befahre ye knew we're 'ere at de cahttage?"

Daniel shrugged his shoulders. "I dink it was ten minutes after ye left de pub. We came in fahr lunch shahrtly after ye two."

Liam added, "De note on de mill was an 'int, too."

As I walked up to Daniel my hand was outstretched but he playfully slapped my attempted handshake away and roughly hugged me, "Anyone dat's a friend o' ooehr lettle sester is family to us! Welcome to de family, Devahn."

I was a little surprised by his exuberant welcome and could only manage, "Thank you!" as I stepped away from our hug.

We all seemed to come together in a small, tight-knit circle beside the mound of supplies that were now in a small four-wheeled cart.

Shavon spoke as she put her arms around both lads, 'Dey call me deir lettle sester because when me mahm died Oi leaned 'eavily ahn dem fahr support. Dey became me family and deir family became me family. Daniel's aunt owns de pub we ate at a cooehple days ago."

Liam smiled, "Lookin' at de supplies we're leavin' ye wit, yahr 'ere just fahr de weekend. Let's do lunch on Mahnday?"

Shavon smiled, "Lunch on Mahnday it is."

Daniel spoke next, "Oi'll leave you wit de cart fahr de weekend. Oi'll pick it up on Mahnday."

Alchemy of the Heart: Shavon Sun Cloud

Shavon offered each of the lads a quick hug. I shook each man's hand, and then they were off to their next delivery. We stood near the cart quietly waiting for the noise of the lory to fade away.

I put my hands on the cart and began to push it down the path. I chuckled as I spoke to Shavon, "Apparently, I passed the test."

"Huh?? What test?"

I smiled, "I was invited for lunch. They didn't ask when I was leaving. That means they think I'm okay and not an immediate threat to you. They want to know more about me."

"Ye got all dat from dat lettle interaction?"

I smugly responded, "Yes," and mentally noted that her accent was thicker again after talking with her friends.

Shavon laughed, "Men. Dey're so complicated!"

It was my turn to laugh. "Men are easy, Shavon. They were checking up on you to make sure you are okay. Daniel was watching my response to you hugging Liam, and Liam was watching my response to you hugging Daniel. They noticed I didn't get jealous, and that I was not threatened by them."

"Which means?"

Alchemy of the Heart: Shavon Sun Cloud

I calmly replied, "Which means, in man-speak, I was not threatening their little sister and I was not some possessive little jerk."

Shavon slowed her pace down, "Fascinatin'."

We spend the next little while putting supplies away and going over the menu. Since I was going to be the quartermaster, I needed to know what supplies we needed.

After we tidied up the cottage, we moved the cart to this side of the creek crossing, close to where I had initially crossed the creek. This was where I had put on my ceremonial clothes for the first time.

Shavon advised me that each person coming to the retreat knew to carry their belongings across the creek and deposit them into the cart. They knew to bathe with the soap we left in the box near the creek, and then dress in their ceremonial clothes. One by one, they would come to the cabin with the cart in ritual silence, drop off their belongings, and return the cart to the creek so the next person could repeat the process. They were to ring a bell if they were unable to bring the cart up due to mobility issues.

Shavon said, 'We may 'ave two, or as many as five people with mobility issues."

I excitedly exclaimed, "Five! How many people do you expect?"

Alchemy of the Heart: Shavon Sun Cloud

Shavon smiled, "We've nineteen women registered, but dere's a standin' invitation for de crones - de elder women - to show up unannounced if dey feel called to attend."

The den mother in me squeaked out, "But what about supper? Will we have enough if more show up?"

Shavon's tone softened, "We always 'ave enough. De crones usually bring food, and many women won't eat a whole pie. Dere's always enough to feed everyone."

Shavon's soft tone and words calmed me down. I asked, "When do the ladies arrive?"

"In perfect divine timin'. Some will arrive early, and some will arrive late. All will be perfect, Devahn."

I could feel a shift in Shavon's entire being - her energy, her presence, and her voice. She stood up, "Devahn, Oi need ye to follow me."

I did what I was told with my now standard, "Yes m' lady."

I followed her to the outhouse, or I should say houses as there were two outhouses side by side. We swept them both out, filled the shelves with toilet paper, sprinkled lime into the pits, and generally made them presentable and usable.

Before we left, Shavon motioned for me to follow her behind one of the outhouses. As a dutiful assistant I followed, and she proceeded to show me that behind the outhouse were a couple of collapsible portable shelters. The shelters were on wheels. We each took hold of one and dragged them out towards the kitchen area.

In a matter of minutes, we opened and placed one of the large shelters over the table and kitchen area to keep us dry if it rained. The second one we set up to one side of the cottage to shelter everyone's belongings. It took a bit longer to set this one up, as there were four sides to hang from the shelter roof.

While Shavon organized her ritual materials, I moved and stacked firewood near the firepit we cooked on, as well as near the firepit near the swimming hole.

When I had finished stacking the wood, I poked my head into the cottage where Shavon was working and spoke, "If we are all done our prep work, I would like to wash up in the creek."

"Excellent idea. May Oi join ye or are ye tired of me company already?"

I couldn't help but smile, "Yes, you can join me. If you ask me this on Monday, though, I may say I am tired of your company. Today, it's still okay!"

Shavon laughed, "Excellent! Devahn, can ye fill de kettle and put it on to boil? Oi'll bring yahr robes and de toiletries in a second."

Alchemy of the Heart: Shavon Sun Cloud

"Yes, m' lady!"

I removed my head from the cottage doorway and as I made my way to the kettle, I heard Shavon's, "Tank ye, m' lord."

I added a couple of small pieces of wood to the firepit and filled the kettle with fresh water. I turned toward the cottage just in time to see Shavon exit the building. She took this shy, small town Florida boy by surprise, again! She was completely naked, except for the roman-styled sandals on her feet. She was wearing nothing else!

Shavon noticed the surprised look on my face and shrugged her shoulders, "Oi didn't want to carry me dirty clothes back."

I was still lightly taken aback by her sheer beauty; the best I could do was shrug my shoulders and offer, "Makes sense. I guess I will do the same."

I headed inside the cottage, took off my clothes and put them into a dirty clothes bag, then proceeded back outside. I didn't have fancy roman sandals, but I did have a set of handy dandy flip flops.

As I closed the door behind me, Shavon was not where I expected her to be. I searched the grounds and saw she was on the other path that led toward the part of the creek were everyone bathes before they come to the cottage. I quickly caught up to Shavon and even before I could ask, she spoke, "We're followin' de same ritual as everyone one else will."

Alchemy of the Heart: Shavon Sun Cloud

All I could do was shrug my shoulders and say, "Yes, m' lady."

After we had bathed and dried ourselves, we headed back to the cottage to dress and have a cup of tea. We sat peacefully for a very long period of time before I heard what I thought was a car door close. Shavon smiled and nodded her head, "In perfect divine timin'. Someone is arrivin'."

Shavon almost whispered to me, "Ground yahrself and be prepared for the onslaught of energies. Dey've been instructed to arrive in silence. Some will, some won't."

Shavon reached over and gently took my hand, indicating for me to stand. She stood in front of me and spoke a prayer, one that she had used many times before.

I was going to have to ask her to translate the Gaelic for me before the next time I heard it.

Alchemy of the Heart: Shavon Sun Cloud

Divine Timing

After the prayer, I could feel the subtleties of the energies in the area change. I could hear more car doors close, and it wasn't long before we heard the rumble and crashing of the first cart coming down the path towards us.

There were a few ladies sitting in silence around the firepit before I heard the gentle ringing of the bell in the distance.

With a slow deliberate pace, I stood and headed to the creek where we left the cart.

Nothing could have prepared me for the initial sight before my eyes! There were half a dozen to a dozen ladies in various states of undress. These ladies varied in age ranging from young maidens to very old crones. This was quite the sight for this young lad from Florida!

A couple of the ladies were slightly embarrassed to be seen naked. My take was that not too many men attended these weekends.

I briefly thought about fleeing the scene, but underneath my panic I knew that was not an option. All I could do was take a deep breath and present a serene calm exterior… in spite of the panic going on inside my head!

Alchemy of the Heart: Shavon Sun Cloud

As the ladies dressed in their ritual costumes, I was impressed. I had never seen so much finery! I felt like I was thrown back in time to the 12th or 14th century. The wardrobe was incredible.

Ritual silence didn't allow us to exchange names, so I slightly bowed to the woman who had rung for help with the cart. I felt great helping this one woman to the cottage. Her energy was so calming, I couldn't help but smile. It was like helping my grandmother.

After my fifth trip back to help another crone with her belongings, I became slightly suspicious that the number of participants in this event was unusual.

As more women arrived, the log benches that served as seats would be rearranged to accommodate another participant. The many long-term participants knew where the components for the benches were stored; even when I was off helping someone come up from the creek, the benches kept appearing. Each time the benches were rearranged in silence a space was made for me to sit next to Shavon.

After the last person arrived, we sat in silence for a long while. Devin version 1.0 was not the most observant person in the whole wide world, but Devin version 2.0 knew without a doubt, he was being eyed up and down. I was being judged and energetically felt into, not so much by the younger maidens, but the crones were doing some serious energy calibration on me. My whole body was tingling. I had no idea what they were up to.

I had to work hard not to completely freak out; my entire fight or flight mechanism was being triggered. I could feel every part of my body being energetically probed. I was feeling almost violated. Yet I sensed no hostile intention behind their probing. It felt more like curiosity and wonderment… but it was still freaking me out!

When Shavon abruptly stood up and commanded, "Enough!" all the probing immediately stopped. My heart rate began to slow down.

Shavon's tone softened, but there was still a command in her voice, "Oi 'ope ye wetches are satisfied and Devahn's passed all yahr testin' and probin'.

It seems word gaht out dat Oi've taken a male apprentice. Oi suspect dats why many o' ye are 'ere dis weekend.

Ye 'll find Devahn to be pure o' 'eart.

Ye'll also find dat 'e's ahnly a nahvice; be patient and gentle if ye find yahrself as 'is teacher.

Let go o' yahr pride if ye find 'im as yahr teacher. He's pure o' 'eart.

Dis weekend'll ahffer many, many learnin's fahr us all as dis is de first time we've 'ad a male in our weekend!"

Alchemy of the Heart: Shavon Sun Cloud

Shavon scanned the participants, feeling into each one. She was searching for any dissension.

The crone whose energy I found so calming when I helped her from the creek stood up and walked over to me with her hands held together, like people do when they pray. She lifted her hands toward me. This was a huge act of recognition. Generally, in Shavon's teachings, the teacher or the master puts their hands over top the student's prayer hands. Uncontrollably, my lip began to tremble. A tear rolled down my cheek as the significance of this woman's symbolic gesture seeped in. I was deeply moved that she was accepting that, at some level, I was going to teach her something.

She gently placed my hands over her worn hands and spoke, "Me name is Caireann. Oi was a student o' Shavahn's mahther, Liadan. All Oi can say is it's damn time we 'ad a male in our circles. Welcome, Devahn."

Then the floodgates opened. I was mobbed with people offering me respect and wanting me to take their hands. I was overwhelmed; tears freely flowed down my face.

After a while, I stopped wiping the tears away as I knew that until the frenzy finished, there would be more tears.

I suspect Shavon sensed the energy in the group shift, so she stood up again and spoke, "Wetches, back to yahr places please." After

Alchemy of the Heart: Shavon Sun Cloud

everyone was in their place she continued, "Devahn is goin' to put de kettle on fahr tea. Den 'e's goin' to look after de paperwahrk dat many o' ye 'ave naht done. Ye'll get yahr chance to know 'im mahre."

A lady that looked very familiar, but not from a previous retreat spoke, "Shavahn, de Friday meals are on yahr vehicle." Once she spoke, I knew who she was. She was Daniel's aunt, the owner of the pub we'd had breakfast at. Her announcement made me happier, since I was not going to have to walk so far to get supper!

Shavon nodded her head in appreciation, "Tank ye."

When all the paperwork was done and payments were collected, we had 38 participants. Shavon secretly told me this was the largest retreat she had ever had at the cottage!

The ages of the women ranged from 22 all the way to 81 years of age. Caireann was the oldest. One of the women that I had surprised at the creek was the youngest.

I thought, "This is going to be an interesting weekend!" I will admit I was slightly terrified.

It took me a few trips to bring the food from the car. Shavon told me she had nineteen registered, but when I carried thirty pies to the cottage, I suspected aunty knew there were going to be more people than Shavon anticipated.

Alchemy of the Heart: Shavon Sun Cloud

I drifted in and out of the lessons as I kept the fire stoked, the teapot filled, and fetched whatever materials Shavon needed for the various lessons.

A couple of times I was working on something when Shavon called me over and I found myself singing with her. In my mind it wasn't necessary, as everyone knew the lyrics to the songs, but when summoned, I did as I was requested!

After one song, Shavon whispered into my ear, "Please get de ingredients fahr mushroom tea, and take out mahre mugs. Ye'll need de 'uge teapaht dat's in back o' de cupboard as well. When it gets dark, we'll 'ave tea!"

I nodded my head in acknowledgement and said, "Yes, m' lady." I saw Shavon smile as I moved away.

It took a long while to organize forty nests into a giant circle inside the cottage while leaving pathways for people to safely get out the door to the bathroom, if need be. Shavon and I found ourselves on either side of the doorway. Shavon figured that if someone was going to get stepped on the way out, it was better us than someone else.

I noticed Caireann was staying close to me. She had a nest on my left-hand side. She playfully apologized to me, "Oi get 'ot and Oi shed blankets."

Alchemy of the Heart: Shavon Sun Cloud

I laughed as I told her, "Me too." I winked as I added, "And I am a swimmer, as well."

Apparently, I said that a little too loud as there were numerous giggles and comments like, "Me too! Oi guess Oi'll see ye in de water." This was followed by more laughter.

I wasn't sure if anyone saw the absolute terror that briefly flashed across my face the very second that I realized that 38 ladies could be seeing 'little' Devin, and that I could be seeing 38 naked ladies of various ages and body sizes. As a rather sheltered boy from small town Florida, I was not accustomed to seeing naked women!

To add to my already rising discomfort, I was aware that most of the 38 ladies were pretty darn good looking, too. The one saving grace was that I was kept too busy to spend much time thinking about it... much. I did say to myself a quick silent prayer, "Whatever you do little Devin, this is not the time to stand out."

Shavon's words brought me out of my temporary state of panic, "When yahr done 'ere let's go outside."

I followed the last woman out of the cottage and stood on the outside of the circle that had informally formed around the kitchen table. Once I arrived, Shavon started giving instructions in her teaching voice, "Once Devahn brings de water over and places it on de kitchen table we'll start ritual silence. We'll remain in silence until de end o' our ceremony. In de unlikely event durin' ceremony dat Oi'm rendered incapacitated, Caireann'll become de ritual leader until de ceremony is over. Is dat understood?"

There was a lot of head nodding and a few women said aloud, "Understood."

Shavon smiled and said, "Good!" then turned to me, "Devahn, will ye please bring de 'ot water?"

I spoke teasingly, "Yes, m' lady." This resulted in a chorus of chuckles.

True to their word, when I set the kettle down the group fell into silence… a silence that was almost deafening.

Shavon made the tea and while it was steeping, they sang two songs that I did not know. I suspected it was an old tongue that I had not had the privilege of learning… yet!

After the echoes of the last melody faded away, the group lined up quietly for Shavon to pour tea into each one's mug. As she did, she gazed deeply into each of the participants eyes, then offered everyone the same blessing, "May yahr journey only be as difficult as de lesson dat'll be shown to ye. May ye accept all de lessons wit grace and ease."

When the last cup had been filled, and the last blessing received, they silently went into the cottage and sat in the safety of their nests.

Alchemy of the Heart: Shavon Sun Cloud

One sole exception was Caireann who, after her mug was filled, quietly moved to stand beside Shavon. When I turned to go into the cottage, Caireann gently yet firmly took hold of my arm, indicating I should stay in place. Shavon simply smiled at the subtle change in protocol and with a slight twirl to the right, stood directly in front of Caireann. With a loving smile that only can be exchanged between a grandmother and her granddaughter, Caireann took the teapot from Shavon.

They stood gazing tenderly into each others' eyes for the briefest of moments. It should be noted that I had not yet touched my tea, or taken any form of drugs, but...

It was like I witnessed many lifetimes of information being exchanged between the two teachers in that moment. I almost had to rub my eyes in disbelief. It was like some magical illusion was playing with my mind. I could swear Shavon was standing in front of Caireann as a twelve-year-old adolescent, not the 32-year-old teacher / maiden / shaman I knew. I breathed in deeply and thought, "The magic of the evening has begun already."

Caireann reached over and tenderly touched my forearm, which broke my silent contemplation. Caireann then spoke to me in the quietest whisper, "Oi can tell yahr aware o' de magic dat's around us. What Oi can't tell ye is what de magic is up to. We 'aven't 'ad a man in a wetches' circle for a very lahng time!"

Alchemy of the Heart: Shavon Sun Cloud

She paused and looked intently into my eyes, "Yahr 'ere fahr a reason, Devahn. Shavon would naht 'ave brought ye tahday if ye were naht meant to be 'ere, or if ye could naht 'andle it. Stay open to what ever 'appens. Keep people safe."

Terror flashed across my face and firmly came to rest behind my eyes. I barely managed to expel a raspy whisper, "What do you mean keep people safe?"

Caireann grinned, "Keep de swimmers from drownin'." She hugged me and turned toward the cottage.

I turned to Shavon. She simply pointed to the door. "We 'ave people waitin'."

Since no further explanation was forth coming, I shrugged my shoulders and headed to the cottage to settle into my nest.

The minute I walked into the cottage I had an uneasy feeling. With only one ritual under my belt, being uneasy was not a great way to start a ceremony.

Shavon led us through the five elements ceremony. She ended the blessing with, "We ask fahr blessin' dat all we do dis evenin' will be true and from de Spirit o' God, de Spirit o' Christ, de Holy Spirit, whoever, or whatever, divine power dwells within ye and ye know to be true."

Alchemy of the Heart: Shavon Sun Cloud

I was startled when I looked into my mug. I only had a couple of sips of mushroom tea left. I either had taken big sips or I didn't get a full mug, and I didn't know which it was.

We sat in silence for a few moments allowing people to settle completely into their nests. When I was fully encased in my nest, Shavon started to sing Snatam Kaur's song, "We are the people…The people of love… Let us people love today."

Shavon only got a few words into the song before everyone, including me, joined in.

We sang the song through a couple of times. Each time we sang it quieter than the previous time. Eventually, at the end of the song, a peaceful silence washed over the entire cottage. I felt a warmth wash over me. It was like a giant blanket of love washed over my entire body.

I don't know how long I was in the sacred cocoon of peace before the hairs on the back of my neck slowly began to rise, followed by the hairs on my arms. This freaked me out a bit… much like the whole evening. I didn't know what was up. I could only take in a deep breath and hold it.

I didn't have to wait for long before all hell broke lose.

I have never heard a person wail like I heard that night, and I hope to never experience that again. It was terrifying, horribly haunting, and completely mesmerizing, all at the same time. It was as if this woman was purging all the hurt and pain she had ever felt in this lifetime - and if you believe in past lives, she was purging those as well. I felt like she was making sure she left nothing out; she was purging all the hurt and pain from her family tree all the way back to Adam and Eve.

I stirred to move towards the woman who was in such agony, when I felt a familiar hand on my arm. Caireann gently pulled me back, indicating I was not to move. This suited me fine as I wasn't sure I currently had the motor skills to navigate my way over to her anyway.

I easily fell back into the safety of my nest. I could hear the stirrings of others. In the darkness I could only assume the wailing woman was being comforted. No words were being spoken but the wailing slowly subsided until it became a slow heartbreaking sobbing. The intensity of the pain coming through her sobbing was extreme. I could feel the grief crashing in on her. I was trying valiantly not to be drawn into her pain, but I was slowly losing the battle. I could feel the tears begin to well in my eyes.

Suddenly there was a spasmatic shift in the energy in the room. I could hear things being throw about and could only assume it was blankets and clothes.

Alchemy of the Heart: Shavon Sun Cloud

Once the thrashing around started, I knew in my heart that a rabbit was about make a run for the swimming hole. I began to untangle myself from my nest. This time Caireann did not try to stop me.

No sooner had I extracted myself from my nest of blankets when a woman ran past me. In the dim cottage light, she appeared to have no pants on. Based on my own experiences with the tea, and conversations Shavon and I had had leading up to the ritual, I was not surprised to see this happen.

I wasn't sure if there would be more. I quickly listened for another rabbit following the first, but there was no sign of a runner. I stepped out of the cottage and quietly closed the door behind me. I turned towards the creek and promptly sprinted like a mad man after the running rabbit.

I caught up to her just as she noisily entered the water. When she was up to her waist in the water, she dove in headfirst and went completely underwater.

I began to take my wool vestments off and piled them neatly while counting very slowly to measure the time that she was underwater… "28… 29… 30… 31…32…33."

I was now naked and moving towards the spot where she dove in, "34… 35… 36…"

Abruptly, she exploded to the surface and joyfully exclaimed for the whole world to hear, "Foehck! It's good to be alive!"

Alchemy of the Heart: Shavon Sun Cloud

She turned towards the shore and froze in her tracks as she spied me standing completely naked and shin deep in the water. Her arms reflexively covered her breasts, then she broke into hysterical laughter. She raucously spoke to herself, "It's a bit late to be cahverin up. 'E's already seen de goods.'

She slowly let her hands drop down by her side and released the tension from her body. She gracefully slid backwards into the water, once again completely submerging her body.

I was still shin-deep in the water when I heard the next rabbit coming down the path.

I was in up to my waist when the third rabbit hit the water.

I lost count after I pulled the seventh person from under the water. Most were as ungrateful as I was when Shavon pulled me to the surface.

They were communing with the fish, the plants... one was even talking with a snail - a very wise snail I was told. The creek seemed rather magical as it was filled with scholarly flora and fauna. No wonder I received such negative responses from those that I hastily pulled up to the surface. They were, as I had been on my first mushroom journey, engaged in enlightening conversations and could not see the need to interrupt their conversations. Drowning was not something that crossed their minds. Drowning had not crossed my mind a couple of days ago, either.

Alchemy of the Heart: Shavon Sun Cloud

If I was under the influence of the mushrooms, it was quickly replaced by my desire to keep everyone safe. I couldn't keep count of how many people were under my care since they appeared to come and go, much like the ebb and flow of the tides.

I was pleasantly surprised and very relieved that little Devin didn't react to the numerous naked bodies that joined me in the creek. I was also very relieved that I did not once feel like a piece of meat as I helped the ladies in and out of the water.

When I deduced that none of the swimmers were under the influence of the magic brew any longer, I quietly asked, "Could you please make your way back to the cottage and see what Shavon has in store for us there?"

Respectfully and quietly, they complied. We soon found ourselves in the cottage where many of the participants were noisily sleeping. I never knew women could snore so loudly!

It didn't take me long to settle into my comfortable nest and it only took a matter of seconds to fall asleep once my head hit the pillow, in spite of the cacophony of sounds from the forty bodies in the cramped cottage.

I was drawn out of my sleep by the same quiet voice that told me to duck when I was blindfolded and walking around the farmyard ducking branches. This time I wasn't ducking branches but sensing that Shavon was awake and stirring. I sleepily peered

Alchemy of the Heart: Shavon Sun Cloud

through my partially opened eyes to verify whether I had sensed correctly. I opened my eyes just a tiny fraction, because I wasn't sure if I wanted Shavon to know I was awake.

As I squinted through the tiny slits of my eyelids, Shavon turned, smiled at me, and mouthed, "Good mornin'."

Surprised and amazed that Shavon knew I was looking at her, I opened my eyes completely. I smiled back, and mouthed back to her, "Good morning."

Slowly I quietly untangled myself from my nest. As I stood, I was suddenly cold. I realized that I was not wearing clothes, but I didn't even blush. I simply rummaged through my nest, found my ritual wardrobe, dressed, and quietly headed out of the cottage to the firepit.

It only took a few moments to get the fire going again. Happy with my handy work with the fire, I went and filled the kettle and placed it over the firepit to heat.

By this time Shavon had stepped outside, too. She waved me over to the outdoor table, where I could see she had already laid out some of the ingredients for breakfast. As I came to stand beside Shavon, she tenderly put her hand on my arm and mouthed, "Tank ye."

I smiled and mouthed back, "You are welcome."

Alchemy of the Heart: Shavon Sun Cloud

She then pointed to her list and indicated for me to bring eggs, bread, and cheese. I nodded my head in understanding and wandered off to the pantry cupboards.

When I returned from the pantry with the ingredients, there was a large group of women outside in various states of undress. It was a little shocking and unusual for this little Florida boy, but at some deeper level of understanding I felt it was okay. This really surprised me.

I tended the fire first and then went to the swimming hole to collect the various clothes that were left on the trail and on the banks of the creek. The rest of the community silently worked together to create a breakfast of veggie omelets, cheese, bread, and tea.

Once breakfast was eaten and we had cleaned up, I filled the kettle again and put it back over the fire. It was then that Shavon broke the silence, "Everyone brin' yahr toiletries and join me at de swimmin' 'ole."

Shavon quietly told me she would bring our toiletries if I would go and set up benches in a circle for the group.

Of course, I dutifully wandered down to the swimming hole and began to hurriedly put benches together for the group. It wasn't that long before everyone was back down at the creek. It probably took longer to get everyone seated and settled than the walk from the cottage to the swimming hole took.

Alchemy of the Heart: Shavon Sun Cloud

Shavon invited everyone to share their experiences of the evening.

Evie had a very difficult time sharing why she was screaming. Once she finally choked out that she was raped two years ago, there was not a dry eye in the circle. This further deepened our visceral experience of Evie's gut-wrenching wailing. It was a sound that I will not forget, ever!

Evie was deeply grateful for all the women that helped console her and move her through her journey. The women that consoled her were grateful for the opportunity to be of service to her.

The first rabbit, errr I mean woman, said, "In 'indsight Oi'm very glad Devahn pulled me to de surface, because Oi surely would've drowned. Oi was so certain Oi could breathe underwater!"

All of the women I pulled up from their underwater communing were extremely grateful… but that didn't mean they wouldn't tease me.

Grace, who was my mother's age, very naughtily said, "Oi've been a widower fahr so long Oi tought de good lord was answerin' me prayers. 'Ere Oi was talkin' wit de plants. Den to me blessed surprise a young, naked man appeared! Me 'ead was underwater and so were 'is manly parts. Let me tell ye, Oi 'adn't been that close to a man's parts in nearly a decade. Oi tought Oi'd died and gone to 'eaven. Dere's no way in dis world Oi'd 'ave de good fortune to be dat close to a naked man while talkin' to a plant!"

Alchemy of the Heart: Shavon Sun Cloud

My face was crimson red as Grace shared her story. Apparently, stepping into the creek naked was not one of my smartest moves, but I didn't want to wear cold wet clothes the next day. That was my story and I stuck to it.

The ladies were not going to let this go and continued to good naturedly tease me. I began to feel like I was one of the lifeguards from the 90's TV series 'Baywatch' who had to strip off his clothes to go in the water. The ladies kept rewinding the recording and reliving it!

After what seemed like an eternal amount of time, Shavon mercifully brought the teasing to an end.

The ladies resumed sharing about the chaos that went on in the room after the swimmers had left. Apparently, anger was the primary emotion and there were a lot of tears shed, as well as some violent pillow punching.

When Shavon sensed that the shares were complete, she adopted her teacher's tone and spoke to the group, "Ye now 'ave free time to wash yahrselves and quietly journal. Ye'll know when it's time to gather."

With that, she stood and easily slipped out of her ceremonial clothing. She picked up her toiletries and walked into the creek without any pomp and pageantry.

Alchemy of the Heart: Shavon Sun Cloud

Since my toiletries were now in the creek with Shavon, all I could do was follow. I pulled my shirt over my head, dropped my drawers, and waded into the water.

After washing and drying myself off, I headed back up to the outdoor kitchen. I quickly prepared tea and gathered the bread and a collection of sweet spreads from the cupboard. I covered up the food so the insects would not get into it, then headed off to bring more wood to the wood pile near the cottage.

I had returned with the third or fourth arm load of wood when Shavon came from the cottage with guitar in hand. I asked, "Do you need me?"

Shavon giggled, "O' course Oi need ye, but right now Oi'm goin' to play me guitar for background music because Oi feel like playin'." She smiled and added, "Devahn, dat was lovely to bring out de tea and bread."

I beamed, "Thank you m' lady!"

Shavon sat down on a makeshift bench near the cottage and began to strum her guitar while I finished stacking the firewood. When I'd completed that task, I snuck into the cottage and tided up everyone's nest as best as I could. I did not know what belonged to who so I was limited in my ability to put things away, but I did a basic tidy. As I was organizing, I could hear the sweet gentle sounds of Shavon's guitar resonate into the cottage.

Alchemy of the Heart: Shavon Sun Cloud

Once I was done, I went back outside and poured cups of mint tea for Shavon and myself. I wandered over and placed her tea near her seat and then sat down with my own tea. Shavon smiled and quietly asked, "Where de 'ell were ye when Oi was actively lookin' for an apprentice?"

Cheekily I responded, "When the master is ready, the apprentice will appear."

Shavon, in the most un-lady like way, snorted and laughed at the same time. "Touché! Well said."

Shavon stopped playing, set her guitar down on the bench, and picked up her tea. She smiled at me and softly spoke, "Devahn, ye don't know how precious ye are. Many men wouldn't 'ave tidied up de cottage or set out tea and bread. Yahr desire to serve in whatever capacity ye can is astoundin' and very much appreciated."

I felt the true sincerity in her words and all I could mumble was, "Thank you m' lady." It wasn't much but it was the best I could offer in the moment.

With a nervous grin on my face and a small catch in my throat I shared, "Truth be told, I was keeping busy so I could process the events so far. I really don't know what you are going to teach and all I can do is respond to what is before me. I struggled with all the nudity, but I responded as best as I could. I don't know the ceremonies, so I can't prepare things before-hand to help you out. Honestly, I am feeling like a fish out of water doing a lot of flopping around."

A single tear trickled down Shavon's face as I uttered the last syllable of my heartfelt confession. She reached over and took my hand. "Devahn, it's when we're faced wit adversity or de unknown dat our true nature rises. Wheder ye know it or naht, dese ladies are watchin' ye and judgin' whether ye 'ave their back and whether dey can truly trust ye. Devahn, de way ye 'andled their teasin' with grace was a test and ye passed wit flyin' colors. Ye scored mahre trust points wit yahr willin'ness to follow me lead and wash up in de creek."

She released my hand and added, "Oi suspect de group is already gahssipin' about de fact ye made a snack and tea fahr dem."

The question in my head, "But how would they know? No one was around when I set out the bread and spreads," must have shown on my face.

Shavon addressed my unanswered question by saying, "Devahn, Oi've never offered tea and a snack. Dey know it was ye and it adds to yahr value."

I had a hard time swallowing because of the big lump that was roosting in my throat. I took a deep breath before I managed to

Alchemy of the Heart: Shavon Sun Cloud

gurgle out, "Thank you." Tears were welling in my eyes, "No one has ever been so nice to me and trusted me this much."

It was my turn to take Shavon's hand. I looked into her eyes and spoke from my heart, "Thank you. Thank you for trusting the universe and seeing something in me that I did not see in me."

"Yahr tankin' me and Oi'm 'umbled and grateful," she replied.

Shavon held my gaze for a long moment before she leaned over and gave me a hug. "Devahn, Oi'm de one who needs to tank ye. Tank ye for trustin' de universe. 'Ad ye naht been open, dis adventure never would've begun. Our relationship would've ended wit a short wheelchair ride. Ye've given me and dese ladies mahre lessons dan ye'll ever know. De last 24 hours alone 'ave been wort de entire price o' yahr ticket."

Tears were now freely streaming down my face as we continued to hug.

I heard an almost silent footstep come up behind me. I don't know how I thought it was Caireann, but I was pretty sure it was her. I felt a gentle hand on my shoulder and as the voice behind me spoke, my suspicion was confirmed.

Caireann quietly offered her praise, "Ye've dahne very well, Devahn. Tank ye fahr lookin' after all de swimmers last night. Now dat mahre trust yah, tahnight should be an interestin' evenin'."

Alchemy of the Heart: Shavon Sun Cloud

I let go of Shavon's hand and turned to face Caireann. She was a sly one! As I turned to face her, I found myself wrapped in a big warm hug. I smiled. It was a warm, tender hug, much like my grandmother used to give me. It was a hug filled with unconditional love and the energy that everything was going to be alright. It was beautiful.

Then just as slyly as she slipped into hugging me, Caireann let her arms slide from hugging me into wrapping Shavon in a loving hug.

Energetically their hug felt like a mixture of motherly and grandmotherly energies.

I wondered, "How do I know any of this? How do I know the difference between grandmotherly energy and an itch in my nose or my spine? Sure, I guessed when the branches were in front of me, but am I lying to myself? Am I making up stories about grandmotherly energy and motherly energy?"

Caireann abruptly interrupted my doubting thoughts as she said with absolute authority, "Yahr naht lyin' and ye do know de difference."

My mouth could have hit the ground with a resounding thump. All I could muster was a bewildered, "What?... How?"

Caireann laughed, "Devahn, yahr surrounded by shamans and wetches. Dis is just de beginnin' o' what we can do."

Alchemy of the Heart: Shavon Sun Cloud

Caireann laughed out loud heartily as she gently took Shavon's face in her withered hands. She kissed Shavon tenderly on her forehead and then turned and headed toward the kitchen, leaving me slightly ungrounded.

I shifted from feeling dumbfounded to feeling playful. I shrugged my shoulders and said, "I think I am going to just go grab my things and see if I can get a ride to the airport. Get out of Ireland, before things get too weird or I end up in jail because I am running down the road naked and high on mushrooms."

Shavon's expression was a little more serious than mine, "Ye'll 'ave to swing by de house and get yahr passport before ye leave."

Then, much like after a great play when the audience erupts into boisterous applause after the last words are spoken and the curtain comes down, Shavon's face erupted into a huge smile.

Shavon's voice took on that teacher tone again, "Caireann is great at plantin' seeds o' possibilities and potential. We're de creators o' our own destiny. It's up to us to decide 'ow we play out our adventures. Tahnight could be crazy, or naht! Don't worry. De truth is, no matter how prepared we are or are naht, it will be what it will be. Oi've learned, to some degree, de more Oi worry de crazier things get. Tings always appear to rise to me anxiety levels. If Oi stay calm, de chaos seems manageable. Oi suggest ye let all

Alchemy of the Heart: Shavon Sun Cloud

yahr worries go and be ready fahr whatever arises." Shavon smiled again, "And know it will all be perfect… even if dere's chaos."

I nervously smiled, "Since I burned my feet I kind of like not having too many surprises."

Shavon mockingly scolded me, "Where's de fun in dat, Devahn?"

I shrugged my shoulders, "I don't know, but it sure feels more comfortable than not knowing."

Shavon laughed, "True, but de real magic in our growth comes from handlin' the unknown."

I did the manliest thing I could think of in the moment. I wrinkled my nose and stuck out my tongue at her like a five-year-old boy. I whined, "Spoil sport!"

Shavon squealed in laughter and then dropped down to my apparent age. She responded as a five-year-old girl with a traditional raspberry, "Tbbbtthhhttt."

I continued in my five-year-old voice, "Don't you have something to do besides spread all your yucky girl germs?"

Shavon stuck out her tongue at me and picked up her guitar. She strummed a few notes, then stuck her tongue out at me again.

I couldn't help but snort. I theatrically stood up and put my hands on my hips. "Shavon Sun Cloud, I am going to tell my mom on you! You were making fun of me!" I turned and ran like a child running to a parent to tattle on a sibling.

I quickly caught up to Caireann. Together we walked to the kitchen to grab a mint tea. I took a new mug because I was not about to go back to Shavon to retrieve my previous mug.

Caireann and I sat down on benches to sip our tea. I suddenly remembered that Caireann could read my mind or pick up my thoughts. The idea of mind-reading could be scary, but for some unknown reason it wasn't. Truthfully, I didn't want to know any more about it in that moment. I just wanted to feel the peace. So, I let go of my thoughts and enjoyed sitting in silence with this wise old crone. It was extremely peaceful listening to Shavon quietly play.

After what seemed like a long while I heard the subtle change in Shavon's playing. She was playing a little bit louder, and the tempo was a bit more upbeat.

Caireann finished her tea and slowly stood to head back to the kitchen area. I did what I was good at and shrugged my shoulders.

I finished my tea and headed over to Shavon. She smiled. There was no tongue sticking out this time. I picked up her now empty teacup as well as my full, cold cup of tea and as I turned to go back to the kitchen, I heard her quiet, "Tank ye!"

I nodded my head to indicate I heard, then carried on to the kitchen area.

Alchemy of the Heart: Shavon Sun Cloud

Into the Unknown

By the time I returned to the kitchen, Shavon was playing louder and singing songs I either did not know or were in Gaelic. Since I couldn't sing along, I busied myself doing what needed to be done - I filled and put the kettle back over the fire. I figured there would be cups to be washed in a few moments.

Slowly, the women began to arrive. The tea and bread drew them to the table first, then they drifted to the area where Shavon was playing. Some sang along with Shavon from the minute they arrived in the kitchen, and some only began to sing after they sat down near Shavon. In all cases, the harmonies were magnificent.

During one magical chant I was absolutely spellbound. I stopped doing the dishes and became entirely lost in the music. Unabashedly, I allowed the tears to roll down my face as I listened to the song. I had no idea what it was about, but it was hauntingly beautiful. It was possibly the most beautiful song I had ever heard in my life.

My eyes were still closed when the song came to an end. I would have been completely startled when I opened my eyes except that I heard a slight shuffle of feet in the dirt just before the music ended.

Even though I had sensed there were people around me, I was still slightly alarmed when I saw the number of women surrounding me. One of the women reached out with her hand towards me, indicating for me to take hold. I tentatively reached out my right hand and took her hand. She gently pulled me forward and we walked hand in hand towards Shavon.

We came to a halt about three feet from Shavon. I was feeling a little awkward as I didn't know what was going on, but I was learning fast to go with the flow!

Shavon abruptly finished playing and handed her guitar to Caireann, who never appeared to be to far from Shavon. Shavon stood up and walked over to stand beside me, taking my left hand in hers. I was desperately trying to remember the name of the woman holding my right had when Caireann rescued me, "It's Kat."

I shook my head in astonishment. Feeling flustered, I managed a quiet, "Thank you."

Standing in front of a whole group of women holding Kat and Shavon's hands I thought, "Can it get any weirder?"

There were only a few seconds before my next thought, "Based on what I have already experienced, it definitely could!'

Much, much worse.

Shavon gently turned to me and quietly spoke, "De last song we sang is called 'Mendin' o' de Soul' in English. Fahr de first time in a very long while, Devahn, we're able to do dis ritual. Dis may be a tad uncomfortable for ye, but please trust us."

I couldn't help but chuckle and questioned out loud, "Getting a little weird?"

Kat and Shavon both laughed. "Devahn, Kat and Oi're goin' to stand 'ere. One o' us will always hold yahr 'and. One may let go yahr 'and but de oeder will 'old on. Is dat okay wit ye?"

I was nervous, yet at some level of understanding I knew whatever was going to take place was going to be safe… for me and the others. So, I nodded my head and spoke quietly, "Yes."

Shavon continued, "Devahn, Oi'm goin' to let go yahr 'and now." As she let go, she continued, "Devahn, yah're goin' to be blindfolded. Dis symbolizes absolute trust. At any point in de ritual, if ye feel uncomfortable or wish to stop, simply let go our 'ands. Is dat understood?"

I responded with more confidence in my voice, "Yes."

Shavon smiled, "Excellent. While yahr blindfolded, ye may feel a woman place 'er 'ead on yahr 'eart, or she may place 'er 'ead gently on yahr chest. Is dat okay? Do all de women 'ave yahr permission to do so?"

This time I responded with authority and confidence, "Yes!"

Alchemy of the Heart: Shavon Sun Cloud

Shavon continued, "Excellent. Oi'm goin' to take hold yahr 'and again and Kat is goin' to let go yahr 'and. She'll tie de blindfold. Is dat okay wit yah?"

I paused before I responded, "Yes, but I do have a question. How long is the ritual? I need to use the toilet if this is going to take any length of time!"

Kat and Shavon laughed in unison. Shavon chuckled as she spoke, "Oi guess we should've asked dat question first."

Shavon let go of my hand and said, "Dis is a great time fahr a toilet break. Let's meet back 'ere in ten minutes."

With that announcement there was a flurry of activity. Seems a lot of us needed to head to the toilet! It was good thing I had put the kettle over the fire; we all had hot water to wash our hands afterwards.

I wasn't sure, but I thought I was back in the seating area around the eight-minute mark. Almost everyone else was already in place, sitting and waiting. Rapidly I scanned the area. We were missing the three star players, Kat, Shavon, and Caireann.

Out of the corner of my eye I spied them coming from the kitchen. I walked back in the spot that I believed was where Kat had originally brought me and waited.

Alchemy of the Heart: Shavon Sun Cloud

As the trio made their way to us, they began singing another song I was not familiar with. The rest of the group knew the song, however, and the harmonies were absolutely spellbinding.

As their song finished, Kat stood on my right side, and Shavon stood on my left side. Shavon took my hand and nodded to Kat. Without a word exchanged, Kat tied a blindfold around my head. A guitar began to play, and I assumed it was Caireann playing.

The collective sang two more songs before I felt a presence in front of me. I don't know how I knew, but it was the same way I knew when there was a branch in front of me and I knew to duck. It was weird. I began to pay attention to my body and felt a little tingling in my solar plexus, like the small jolt you get when you stick your tongue on a 1.5 v battery. Yes, I was the guy that stuck my tongue on a battery. I even stuck my tongue on 9V battery once. I never did that one again!

I was nervous, and my mind was rocketing all over the place. Energetically, I was a train wreck and I suspected I was not really helping the women in the exercise. Once I realized this, I was horrified. I was here to help. I felt like a child caught with his hands in the cookie jar.

All I could do was take a few deep, slow, cleansing breaths. This slowed my thought processes, and I began to center myself. I allowed myself to expand. I allowed my presence to grow. I felt the air around me. I felt the sensation of my feet in my shoes, and my shoes on the ground. I felt the sun on my bare arms. I smelled the fragrances in the air. I sensed my toes expand. I sent imaginary roots into the earth and mixed them with the roots of the grass. My roots extended beyond the grass and out into the trees. My roots, the grass roots, and the tree roots became one. I felt the sun on my entire body. I was calm and centered.

I felt like I was standing taller now in front of the collective. I was more aware of the presence of another woman in front of me. Then she stepped away and another stood in front of me. The women each took a turn standing in front of me. I could feel the difference between each one. For some, I felt their reluctance to stand in front of me. For others, I sensed their energetic challenge to me. For some, I felt an acute sense of distrust. No matter who stopped in front of me, all I could offer was my stoic presence and unconditional love for them.

Judging from the occasional muffled sob, this was exactly what was needed.

A few women put their hands on my chest, right where my heart was and felt into my energy, which was open and non-threatening.

I knew without a doubt when it was Evie standing in front of me - her energy was alive and very hostile. I was also keenly aware that she had two women with her. I could only surmise it was for support. She stood there unmoving for a long time. I could feel her hostility through her energy and her breathing.

I told myself, "This woman needs all the love you can muster, Devin. Now is the time to let it shine and flow through."

I felt my arms grow heavier at my sides as I relaxed even more. I softened the front of my chest to open myself. I did my best to wordlessly express more love.

Suddenly, my left hand shot up and caught Evie's right hand mid-slap. I almost breathed a sigh of relief as I held her hand. The slap would have hurt a lot had she connected. I moved her right hand to my face. She did not resist as I placed her hand on my face. Her hand was there for a few moments before I sensed the subtle shift in her energies. My right hand bolted upwards and intercepted her left hand. I caught her hand and then slowly moved it to my face.

After a few moments with both of her hands on my face, I moved her right hand back down to her side and let go. After a time, I did the same with her left hand.

It did not take long before her right hand rocketed back up toward my face. Once again, I intercepted her swing and brought her hand slowly to my face.

This exercise carried on for a long time. First her right hand, then her left hand. Each time, I intercepted her swing and gently placed it on my face. Over time I noticed that her swings were less and less angry and contained significantly less energy. While this was going on, the collective continued to sing and hold space for Evie.

Then it was like the dawning of a beautiful new day. I felt like I had a giant explosion in my brain, and then I was crystal clear. The next time Evie went to hit me, I was to allow it. I was very aware I was not going to like it, but to help Evie heal I needed to do this. I also needed to remember that this was not personal. This was not about me. This was about helping a friend who needed closure.

I moved Evie's right hand back down off my face. Both of her hands were at her side. I felt her energy shift into the frustration of the complete unfairness of the situation in her life. Her energy became frenzied. She didn't deserve what had happened to her. Life was so unfair! She hated her life.

I knew it was coming. I don't know how I didn't flinch when she slapped me as hard as she could with her right hand, but I didn't. My face hurt. It hurt a lot. My blindfold was knocked cockeyed, but I stood there. It was crystal clear to me that I needed to love Evie even more, despite what just happened, despite how sore my face was… and would be for the next little while!

Inside I was smiling, knowing that I would take a beating if needed to support Evie.

The second I had the thought that I would take a beating for Evie's healing was the exact second I heard her sob. She cried out in anguish and buried her head into my chest. I felt Kat and Shavon let go of my hands. I knew what Evie needed now was for me to simply stand there and hold her.

Evie sobbed uncontrollably while I held her for a long time.

As her tears began to subside, I felt her entourage move in to encircle us.

Moments later, I felt and heard people moving toward us. I was still blindfolded, but I could sense the number of arms around us and feel the warmth of the bodies engulfing us in love. "So, this is a group hug!" I thought to myself.

After a few moments together, a spontaneous collective sway began to happen. Various women unexpectedly sobbed. I could hear crying. I did not really understand what was going on, but I knew I needed to stay present in the here and now.

We collectively swayed and cried together for a very long period of time. The last time I felt this connected to a group was when I was twelve years old at summer camp. I was a junior counsellor, and I spent the whole summer with the same group of friends. As all young kids would do at the time, we swore on sacred spit handshakes that we would always be friends… friends forever.

Forever did not turn out to be very long in my case. For some, the sacred friendships lasted for a year. The shortest one was only a couple of weeks into the start of school. Apparently, I wasn't cool enough outside of summer camp to be their friends.

I carried the hurt of the lost friendships for many years... possibly still even now.

It was my stomach's sudden and extremely loud grumbling that caused a wave of giggling and laughter to wash throughout the entire collective. This effectively changed the energy to, "Oi'm 'ungry, too. Dis was beautiful, but what's fahr lunch?"

There were still many hugs as I was slowly allowed to unravel from the group. I even got a few kisses on the cheek before they all left with Shavon to head back to the kitchen.

Kat stood beside me for the entire time, ensuring I was safe. Or so I thought. Once everyone was gone, Kat turned to me and gave me a massive, warm, loving bear hug. She tearfully spoke, "Tank ye fahr trustin' de process, trustin' me, fahr bein' so open, and allowin' dis ritual to 'appen. Ye may never know de 'uge impact ye've 'ad on dese women, and me life. Tank ye!"

I was a bit flabbergasted by her sudden emotional declaration. I did the only thing that felt right to do in the moment - I hugged her back and replied, "You are welcome, Kat, and thank you for having my back."

Kat took hold of my hand, and we walked toward the kitchen. Just before we reached the kitchen table, she let go of my hand, kissed me on the cheek, and said, "Tank ye!" Then she slipped into the collective mass of women.

After being part of what I could only describe as a mosh pit of warm affectionate energy, I suddenly felt very alone. Alone... and very thirsty.

Within minutes of that realization, Caireann appeared with a glass of water with a slice of lemon floating in it. She held the glass in front of my face and commanded, "Drink!"

I grinned, and dutifully did as commanded. I was about to playfully respond when a small lump in my throat suddenly appeared, making it difficult to speak. "Caireann, I don't have a grandmother. I have no family other than my mother... and now Shavon. May I call you Grandmother?"

I waited for her response with a mixture of fear that she would say no and dread that I may have hurt her feelings.

I didn't have to wait long before Caireann's face lit up like the fireworks on the Fourth of July. She was beaming from head to toe as she excitedly spoke, "O' course! Oi'm grandmahther to everyone 'ere. Oi'd lahve ye to call me Gran." She gave me a grandmotherly hug that almost melted me to the core! I was falling even more madly in love with this woman by the second.

Alchemy of the Heart: Shavon Sun Cloud

I just finished drinking the glass of water when Caireann literally ripped the glass from my hand. She commanded, "One mahre glass, and den yah're comin' wit me to de ritual change place."

I smiled, then impishly grinned, "Yes, Gran."

Caireann beamed as she headed back to the kitchen with my glass. She returned a few moments later, the glass filled with water and more lemon. I was a bit perplexed. I had helped put the groceries away and I didn't remember unpacking any lemons. Without prompting Caireann offered, "I brought dem and a few ahder tings as well."

I hoped Caireann's comment was because she saw the perplexed look on my face, and not that she was somehow reading my mind again.

I drank my water as commanded and said, "I will meet you there, Gran. I need to use the bathroom."

Caireann nodded her head. She spoke in a gentle tone, "Give me ten minutes and den come. Dere'll be ahders dere wit me!"

I nodded my head to indicate I understood, then I left my water glass in the kitchen and fled to the outhouse. The two large glasses of water drunk in a very short time was stretching my bladder!

I waited for what I thought was ten minutes before I headed back towards the cars and the area where I suspected everyone bathed and changed into their ritual clothing. As I got closer, I could hear gentle chanting.

I arrived to find Caireann and two of the more elderly ladies chanting. They were standing around a small clay bowl with what appeared to be spruce needles and something else in it. What ever it was, it was very smoky and very fragrant.

I was rather surprised that Caireann was wearing a headdress made of antlers, possibly deer antlers. One of the other ladies wore a headdress of feather and fur. The third lady's face was painted with a giant red streak that ran from the top of her head to the bottom of her chin.

Caireann also held a giant, ornately carved staff in her right hand. The top of the staff looked all twisted and gnarly. I swallowed and thought, "Oh shit, Devin! What the hell did you get yourself into here?"

Despite the fear raging through my mind, screaming at the top of its figurative lungs, "Devin, are you crazy!? You don't know what cult you're getting yourself into! Maybe they'll drug you and make you their sex slave or boy toy! You've heard talk of the appetite of women in the seniors' lodges," I continued to walk toward the group.

Caireann did nothing to help ease the discomfort arising in my stomach when she commanded, "After de last ritual, ye need energetic clearin'. Ye need naht take ahn energy o' de ladies. Take ahff yahr clothes. Take as lahng as ye need to wash yahrself in de creek and den come back. Dis might be embahrssin fahr yah, but dahn't put yahr clothes back ahn until we smoehdge ye. Our smoehdge is made up o' pine and juniper, as well as tyme and a lettle sage. It's naht de same as de sage yahr Nahrth American Indians use, but it's sage."

My little mind was whirling away, "What the hell is smudge? Maybe that's how they are going to drug me! Why the hell am I doing this?"

Despite the raging in my head, I stripped off my woolens and walked into the creek. I waded over to the other bank where the cleansing soap was stored. I pulled the soap from the box and walked back into the creek.

I was just beginning to wash when I heard a gentle little splash behind me. I didn't even have to turn around to know it was Caireann. She carefully walked into the creek to stand in front of me wearing her full ceremonial garb. She spoke gently to me, "Devahn, yahr a powerful young man. Oi know tings are crazy in yahr mind right now. Ye need to ground. Stay focused. We understand we're askin a laht o' ye. Many tings are flyin' at ye out o' nowhere. We've put ye into de deep end o' de pool witout any instructions or description o' what's goin' ahn. Oi want ye to know, yahr doin' great, but we need ye to trust Shavahn and yahr Gran.

Alchemy of the Heart: Shavon Sun Cloud

Know we're naht askin ye to do anythin' illegal, or immahral. Ye and Shavahn'll 'ave plenty o' time over de days fahllowin' dis gatherin' to discuss de significance o' de rituals and what 'as gone ahn."

She smiled and added, "It's been years since dis many crones 'ave gathered and even lahnger since dis group o' crones 'as gathered. Know dat dis is a truly magical day!"

The only thing I could do was smile, shrug my shoulders, and say, "Okay." I proceeded to ground myself.

Caireann smiled, "Tank ye!" and then waded through the creek toward the other crones.

Once I completed washing up, I headed towards the group, as well.

In a language I didn't understand, the woman with the red painted face proceeded to lift the small pot of smoking pine needles and other herbs and wave it around my body. She ensured that all of me was completely covered in smoke. This, in my mind, completely undid the cleanliness of my washing up.

She uttered words that I suspected were some form of incantation as she moved the pot around my body. I sensed the words were very old. Was I making this up in my mind or was there truth to it? I would have to remember to ask Shavon after the weekend was done.

Alchemy of the Heart: Shavon Sun Cloud

The woman smudging me stepped away, still holding the smudge pot in her hands.

It appeared that this was the cue for the woman with the fur and feather headdress to step forward and speak, "Devahn, fahr yahr sake, because dere were many people ye were introduced to at de beginnin', me name is Fiona. Me sester dat smoehdged you is Bredget.

You washed yahr bahdy in de creek to cleanse yahr physical bahdy. Me sester smoehdged ye wit smoke to clear and balance yahr energetic bahdy in a purifyin' ritual. Devahn, Oi…"

Fiona paused and looked to her left and right, extending her arms to include the other two women, "We want ye to know 'ow impressed we were wit yahr 'andlin o' de masculine energy exercise. Trust me when Oi say dis wasn't planned. Kat's intuition told 'er it would work. Shavahn and Caireann supported it, but it was naht ahn de schedule."

I blurted out in an exasperated tone, "There's a schedule?"

Fiona's face lit up as she laughed, "Naht a printed schedule, but mahre a tradition. 'Arder tings are done on dese weekends. Yahr presence provided de group wit a unique ahpportunity. We've very few men followin' our druidic traditions. Dere are male druids in de world, but in our lineage, we've naht 'ad many male followers. In our traditions nahdin 'as ever been written down and

Alchemy of the Heart: Shavon Sun Cloud

is only passed down wit stories and experiences. Druidry's been around since de times o' de romans and many generations before. Druidry went underground at de time o' Christianity and de purge o' de pagan religions. What we – dis collective group o' women - practice now, is de 'onourin' o' nature, de oneness o' Gahd – de power dat makes all tings, includin us. Many o' de women are still active in de Catholic church. Our traditions are meant to enhance all faiths in de oneness o' Gahd. We use traditional costumes and wardrobe as a symbahlic way to bring us back to our roots and to cahnnect us back to nature."

Fiona raised her hand to quieten me before I could ask her a question or make a statement. She continued, "Caireann is de 'igh priestess o' dis whole collective. She initiated Shavahn's mahther, Liadan, Shavahn, and Oi. Oi believe Caireann initiated almost 'alf o' de women in de circle. Shavahn 'as natural charisma and leadership skills. Shavahn is mahst actively promotin' and sharin' de teachin's. She is, to mahst people, de face o' de group. Caireann is de elder and 'igh priestess. She's de symbahlic 'ead. In trut, she 'as a far greater role because she 'olds de energy and de intention o' de teachin's.

As tings evolve and new ways o' tinkin come to light, we brin' dese learnin's and new methods back to de circle. Dis is why we are druid, yet naht known as traditional druids."

Fiona paused to let all she had told me sink in.

Alchemy of the Heart: Shavon Sun Cloud

I remained attentive and she continued, "Oi'm tellin' ye all dis, so ye understand dat Shavahn is big in our tradition. She's a true leader and dis whole community is behind 'er.

Shavahn did naht orchestrate what comes next. Dis was de community gatherin' together after ye did so well in de masculine energy exercise." She smiled and added, "Yahr fishin' expedition de last night was also well done.

De community would like to fahrmarly welcome ye into de family. To do dat, we 'ave a small sacred ritual. Ye'll be 'appy to know dat it does naht include cuttin' off any o' yahr manly parts."

Nervously I laughed and said, "That's good!" With a bit of hesitation, I asked, "Can you tell me what this ritual *does* entail?"

Fiona smiled, "Oi can naht, but know it's notin' dangerous and it does naht entail brandin', tattooin', or any permanent exterior markin'. Ye may, however, carry de energy o' de welcomin' witin yahr 'eart fahrever!"

Again, Fiona raised her hand to silence the question that was forming in my head.

I nodded my head and Fiona continued, "Oi'll present ye to de 'igh preistess, Caireann. Bredget'll ask ye if ye wish to join de community. Yahr free to answer wit eider "yes" or "no". Eider answer is acceptable. If ye choose no, dat is totally fine. We'll 'onour yahr decision. If ye choose yes, Oi'll ask ye de same question, "Do ye wish to join de community?" Wance again only answer wit "yes" or "no"! If yahr in any doubt, de correct answer is "no".

If ye say "yes", de 'igh priestess'll ask ye fahr a tird and final time, "Do ye wish to join de community?" Wance again, "yes" or "no" are de only acceptable answers. If ye say "yes" fahr a tird time, we'll begin de ritual.

We've cleansed yahr bahdy and cleansed yahr spirit so dat intuition can cleanly guide ye to de answer dat supports ye.

Dere is no ahbligation fahr ye to say yes. Do ye understand? Do ye 'ave any questions?"

I grinned playfully, "Yes, to the first question. No, to the second question."

Fiona smirked, knowing I was teasing by answering in only yes/no answers. "Great! Let's continue."

It was Bridget's turn to speak. In a very authoritative voice, much like a judge reading the charges to a criminal before they are sentenced, she said, "Devahn, witout knowin' all de details o' what yahr acceptance in de community could invahlve, only knowin de 'eart and intentions o' yahr sponsor, Shavahn Sun Cloud, would ye like to become a member o' dis sacred group?"

Alchemy of the Heart: Shavon Sun Cloud

The wording was different from what Fiona led me to believe was going to be asked, but I understood the intentions were the same. I also knew in my heart, regardless of the lack of details, that I was not joining some diabolical group intent on harming the world.

My musings were interrupted by a giant firecracker that went off in my mind, a huge explosion of understanding. The instantaneous flash of insight literally dropped me to my knees.

I now completely understood why Shavon dropped a package off to someone she didn't know. It was because it was a sister from her group that asked her! It may possibly have been one of the women at this very retreat.

In that flash of insight, I was utterly mentally fried. Friends asked me once to help them move and I said no, just because it was inconvenient. I didn't feel like helping them, so I didn't!

The thought of having friendships that were as deep as the friendships these women shared scared the hell out of me. To be the kind of friend that would delay a flight and go to another city to drop off something for you was a concept I had not been able to fathom.

I must have had wild eyes, like I had just seen a ghost or my own mortality, as all three women stepped forward and gently touched me on the shoulders.

Alchemy of the Heart: Shavon Sun Cloud

It was Caireann that spoke, "It's truly scary and almahst unimaginable when ye begin to see de depth o' de friendships dis group 'as created, isn't it?"

I had a lump the size of a watermelon in my throat. It seemed impossible to answer the question with nothing but a yes or no answer. I had so many questions, concerns, and ideas swimming in my head. I was figuratively drowning in a sense of unworthiness.

I opened my mouth to speak, but I could not make a sound. In frustration, I closed my mouth and opened it again. Again, nothing came forth.

Caireann spoke in a gentle soothing timbre, "Oi dahn't know if dis'll make it worse or better fahr ye but de 'ole group tinks yahr worthy. No matter what ye tink, ye've nearly 30 new friends who're willin' to support ye... especially de tree dat are standin' in frahnt o' ye right now!"

The thought of Shavon and Caireann being my lifelong friends was very comforting. The thought of twenty-eight other lifelong friends made me feel overwhelmed. Caireann's words did not help.

Caireann could tell I was still in fear. She chuckled softly, "Devahn, Oi understand de overwhelm. Oi ask ye to be open to de concept of 'aving deep friendships. It dahn't mean ye 'ave to 'ave any wit' any one o' us. Many women 'ere ye'll never see again.

Be open to de ahpportunity to support someone if ye choose to do so. Dere is no law or bond to say ye 'ave to say yes to any request. We simply ask ye to be open to sayin' yes."

With those last words, my heart finally stopped beating one million miles an hour and the sense of overwhelm eased. I was able to breathe normally again.

Fiona and Bridget both smiled now. They could see that I was finally getting the concept. I was settling into the fact that I could be okay with being part of a group that had such deep friendships.

The racket in my head cleared away. The lump in my throat suddenly vanished, and I was able to swallow completely again. I stood noticeably straighter. The decision was easy.

I declared emphatically, "Yes!"

The instant I gave Fiona my answer, a flash of realization nearly blinded me, like a flash bulb on a camera. A tsunami of grief and shame washed over me. All my life my love had been entirely conditional, without exception. Even my love, I was horrified to admit, for my own mother. If she didn't do what I wanted or needed, I withheld love.

Alchemy of the Heart: Shavon Sun Cloud

Love, to me, was a tool I used on everyone. No wonder I didn't have friends! Many people tried to befriend me, but I drove them away with my spoiled two-year-old mentality about love. I used my conditional love as an instrument, rather like a lumberjack with a sharp axe cutting wide swaths in the forest of people around me, taking massive chunks out of each person.

When I first met people, I was friendly to them, but then I turned into a venomous snake, poisoning all my relationships with the attitude, "If you don't do this for me, I won't share love and affection with you." In this moment I was disgusted by this realization and deeply ashamed.

The misery didn't stop there. In the span of a tenth of a second, my whole life flickered before my eyes. I saw things about myself that I am sure many people only see on their death bed. I hated the parts of me I was seeing. I was an ugly cruel person.

The massive weight of these realizations dropped me to my knees in a spasming, crumpled heap.

I sobbed and bawled, reliving all the experiences that showed me all the ugliness I was. I lost all track of time.

I have no idea how long I lay on the ground and cried but I became vaguely aware that Caireann had sat down on the ground beside me. At any given time she was either holding me in a tender embrace or was holding my hand.

Fiona and Bridget each took turns sitting with me, as well.

When I was finally able to stop sobbing and return to the present moment, I was shocked to see it was now dark. The trio of supporting women had me surrounded. Somehow, they were sitting in chairs.

I felt lighter without the weight of seeing the way I had been, but I also felt exhausted. I hoarsely croaked, "Can I get a drink of water?"

Caireann tenderly smiled at me like a loving grandmother who had just witnessed someone she loved go through hell. "Sorry, Devahn. We fergot water… but we 'ave tea!"

As I spoke, I felt my parched throat crackle, "Bit early for magic tea, isn't it?" The trio screamed in delight!

Fiona spoke, "Oi tink ye'll naht be drinking magic tea for a o' couple days. Ye need time for what ye experienced to settle in."

Bridgett handed me a cup and said, "It's warm lemon water and 'oney."

I gratefully took the cup and offered her a heartfelt, "Thank you."

The warm drink felt like pure bliss, like ice cream on a hot day! Soothing and totally refreshing.

Alchemy of the Heart: Shavon Sun Cloud

I sat comfortably amidst the trio of elders and sipped my lemon water.

When I felt more grounded, I asked, "What the hell was that?"

Caireann spoke, "Great question, Devahn. De short answer is ye 'ad an epiphany, or as some people call it, an awakenin'."

I was puzzled, "An awakening? Awakening of what?"

Caireann softly replied, "Dat's a question ye 'ave to answer yahrself, Devahn. What was it ye saw about yahrself that was so horrible it caused ye to collapse?"

I was genuinely surprised as I began to share what I experienced. My throat didn't close, and there was no big lump that formed.

"I saw the way I was. I saw that I only loved people conditionally. People tried to be friends, but I chased them away. I used love as a tool…"

I paused and took a deep breath before I could continue, "I saw that I used love as a tool, even with my own mother."

With a tone of disgust, I repeated, "I used conditional love with my own mother!" I sobbed again, "My own freaking mother!"

Caireann touched my shoulder and lovingly spoke, "We've all done tings we're ashamed and disgusted wit'. When yahr ready, tell us more bout yahr experience."

Alchemy of the Heart: Shavon Sun Cloud

I took a few deep breaths and attempted to recenter myself. I sighed heavily, took a few slower, deep breaths, and grounded myself before I could continue to speak, "I had this realization that I was a horrible person. It was meeting Shavon that was the catalyst for me to change. She was so different from me. She loved openly and unconditionally, which was a foreign concept to me. Completely foreign. Completely out of my wheelhouse.

Then I met you all, and I guess it just blew my circuitry and tripped a breaker?"

Fiona inquisitively asked, "Tripped a breaker?"

I chuckled and offered an American-to-Irish translation, "I blew a fuse."

The trio nodded in collective understanding. Caireann spoke, "Dat's a good description. Ye tripped a breaker. When yahr old tought patterns get destroyed because o' a new way o' tinking, it's like a reset.

Devahn, ye'll never be able to go back to de old way. Yahr neuropathways 'ave been rewritten. Oi'd say ye 'ad a spiritual awakening, an awakening o' de 'eart."

"And my dear friend, Shavon Sun Cloud, had a direct influence on my Heart Awakening. If she would not have gone to Florida, I would be none the wiser." I playfully added, "So, this is all her fault."

Alchemy of the Heart: Shavon Sun Cloud

Caireann playfully messed up my hair. "If it were only dat simple. De trut is Devahn, ye said yes, every step o' de way. Sayin' yes at every step indicates ye no longer blame others. Ye start bein' accountable fahr yahr own life." She pointed at me, "Yahr makin' the changes yahr seekin'."

I grinned playfully at Caireann, "It is still easier to blame others."

Caireann laughed, "At times it is."

Caireann paused, gathered her thoughts, and then asked, "Ye comfortable down dere on de ground?"

I snorted, "Surprisingly enough, I am."

"Grand. Bridget, would ye start de questions again?"

Bridget smiled and nodded her head. "Devahn, witout knowin' all de details o' what yahr acceptance in de community could invahlve, only knowin de 'eart and intentions o' yahr spahnsor, Shavon Sun Cloud, would ye like to become a member o' dis sacred group?"

My heart skipped a beat in pure excitement. Almost shouting, I exclaimed, "Yes!"

I turned slightly to face Fiona a bit better. A smile splashed across Fiona's face, "Devahn, witout knowin all de details o' what yahr acceptance in de community could invahlve, only knowin de 'eart

251

Alchemy of the Heart: Shavon Sun Cloud

and intentions o' yahr spahnsor, Shavon Sun Cloud, would ye like to become a member o' dis sacred group?"

Beaming like a kid at an awards ceremony who just won the award for best student, I replied emphatically, "Yes!"

I expectantly turned to face Caireann whose face had to be hurting because she was smiling so wide, and she asked, "Devahn, witout knowin all de details o' what yahr acceptance in de community could invahlve, only knowin de 'eart and intentions o' yahr spahnsor, Shavonn Sun Cloud, would ye like to become a member o' dis sacred group?"

As the last syllables rolled off her tongue, a feeling of total acceptance was imbued in every cell in my body. In response, I spoke a holy, yet quiet, "Yes!" A tear rolled down my cheek.

Caireann let go of my gaze and carefully pushed herself out of her chair. Bridget and Fiona did the same. Then they all shuffled to stand in front of me.

Caireann's demeanor changed. She was once again the elder, the teacher, the keeper of the lineage and history. This matriarch of the group spoke, "Devahn, each one o' us in de group uses de surname of Sun Cloud. We belong to de greater order o' de Clouds.

Alchemy of the Heart: Shavon Sun Cloud

'Clouds' represent many tings - hope, purity, transformation, change, enchantment, and mystery. All o' which we strive to live and uncover in our spiritual transformation.

De 'Sun' represents life, but it's also known to typify energy, power, positivity, and clarity. De sun is a natural force dat's outside our control. It also illuminates de world around us, helps livin' creatures navigate the planet, and sustains many essential ecosystems.

We each come to understand what de two words mean to us. It's our collective knowledge that deepens our bond.

Devahn, de council before ye 'as recognized yahr pledge to join de group. We accept it was freely given and witout any 'idden motive.

Derefore, it's de wish of dis council to grant ye full membership into de community.

Devahn, witout knowin' what it would entail, would ye 'onour us in the next step of full membership into dis group?"

I took a moment to look deeply into each of the elder's eyes. I was moved to tears as I saw strength, love, and compassion at a depth and level I had never seen in these women before. As tears streamed down my cheek, I responded with a heartfelt, "Yes!"

Alchemy of the Heart: Shavon Sun Cloud

It was Fiona who spoke, once again, as the master of ceremonies, the Sergeant at Arms, "Devahn, ye'll wait 'ere. We'll send an escort party to take ye to de ceremony, a celebration. We ask ye to remain in silence until yahr asked to speak. It'll be Caireann who'll ask ye to break yahr silence. Is dat understood?"

I nodded my head in agreement and reverently spoke, "I understand."

Then, without further adieu, the trio left me standing alone. I could hear them walking the path toward the cottage.

When I could no longer hear them, I ran to hide behind the nearest tree. The necessities of the physical body were long overdue. I think I heard my bladder take a deep audible sigh of relief.

I didn't know how long I would have to myself, so I quickly ran into the creek. I retrieved the soap from its box and quickly washed off the dirt from my little roll around on the ground.

It was not long after I put the soap back and allowed myself some time to drip dry, and dress in my ceremonial clothes again that I saw six torches heading my way. The scene could play out in my overactive imagination as something ominous. There were six women with very serious looks on their faces headed my way in ritual garb. The last time I saw such a serious face on a woman, my mom was after me to give me a spanking for breaking one of her favorite ornaments. She had told me hundreds of times not to

Alchemy of the Heart: Shavon Sun Cloud

play with them, and based on my new information about my past, I may very well have broken that ornament out of spite. I thought, "When I get home, I really must apologize to her for breaking it."

My escort party arrived. Some were wearing headdresses made of goat horns or deer antlers. Some wore headpieces decorated with feathers. All of them had painted faces and a long spear in one hand. They held a torch in the other hand. They held an air of 'warrior'.

I wasn't keen to find out if they knew how to use their spears, or whether they were entirely ceremonial.

One of the ladies spoke, "Fahllow behind us two to tree feet!" I recognized the voice, but with the blur of the last day and everything I just went through, I wasn't sure who it was.

I shrugged my shoulders and stepped in behind them. I assumed, based on watching old movies with Knights and stuff, that they were my honor guard.

We walked to the cottage and continued past it towards the swimming hole. I could now see that there were a bunch of torches. The women appeared to be gathered in a circle.

As we got closer, I noted that I was sort of correct, as the women were actually standing in a horseshoe shape. The council of elders stood at the top of the horseshoe. Off to the right-hand side, Shavon stood in her full ceremonial regalia, wearing her green skirt, white top, and a green shawl. The honor guard walked me to Shavon.

Without speaking Shavon waved to me, indicating to follow her. Dutifully, I followed. She led me to the top of the horseshoe, and we stopped directly in front of the council of elders.

Caireann, Fiona, and Bridget all smiled. As foretold, it was Caireann who spoke, "It's been many years since we've 'ad de ahpportunity to invite a new member into de circle. Who brings fort dis new member to de circle?"

Shavon spoke, "Oi, Shavahn Deidre Aislin Sun Cloud, do bring dis new member to de circle!"

Caireann continued to smile, "Who is dis new member?"

Shavon heralded my name, "Devin Alexander Jones." I was impressed on two counts. One, she managed to drop the Oirish accent off my name, and two, she remembered my full name. I think the only time I shared my whole name with her was for the purchase of my plane ticket.

Caireann continued, "Does anyone in de circle ahbject to admittin' Devahn Alexander into de circle?"

There was complete silence from the group. Caireann allowed a few moments of silence to pass before she continued. I assumed

Alchemy of the Heart: Shavon Sun Cloud

she was giving people enough time to respond if they chose to do so.

Caireann spoke again, "Devahn Alexander, do ye ahbject to joinin' de circle as a full family member and dedicatin' yahr time and energies, as available, to learnin' de ways of de circle?"

I proudly and boisterously responded, "I do not object. I willingly and freely choose to join the circle and learn the ways of the circle."

Bridget stepped forward and as she did a small container of blue paint appeared from behind her back. She dipped three fingers into the paint and then placed them just below my left eye and streaked them down towards my chin. I could feel the cool paint on my cheek. Bridget declared, "Ye now bear de mark o' de Clouds."

Bridget stepped back. Fiona stepped forward and took from her pocket a silver chain with a five-fold amulet. Fiona hung the chain around my neck and spoke, "Ye now wear de symbol of Druidry. If yahr ever lost, de symbol will provide ye wit de way home."

Fiona stepped back. Caireann stepped forward and without any preamble or warning, she slapped me hard across the face, "Every newborn is slapped at birth to brin' on de first breath. Wit dat slap, Devahn, ye've been reborn into a new way o' bein'. Yahr now Devahn Alexander Sun Cloud."

Alchemy of the Heart: Shavon Sun Cloud

Using only hand motions, Caireann indicated for me to turn and face the horseshoe. Dutifully, I complied.

Fiona proclaimed from behind me, "Oi present to ye our brahder, Devahn Alexander Sun Cloud."

Then, like flies on a piece of meat near the barbeque, they swarmed me. Each person in turn welcomed me to the circle and shared their full name with me.

I don't know when the music and dancing started, but I was extremely aware when the sun began to rise. We all turned to the east and drank in the beauty of the sunrise. I don't think I had ever stayed up all night and saw a sunrise before!

My feet and body were stiff and sore from dancing all night. My throat was raw from singing; everyone had to teach me a song and/or they wanted to sing with their new brother. At first, I was reluctant to join in, but eventually, I said, "What the hell!" and sang with everyone and every request.

That night was possibly the most fun I had ever had in my whole life! I know I will NEVER forget it.

After witnessing the sunrise, Shavon moved over and stood next to me. As we stood watching the sunrise, she placed her hands on my bicep and tenderly spoke, "Ye 'ad a big day yesterday. Tank ye fahr bein' so acceptin' of it all."

I replied equally as tenderly, "Yes, it was a big day. Thank you for taking a chance on me on that fateful day in the hospital."

Shavon chuckled, "Oi was takin' a package to Caireann's granddaughter. She was de one Oi was 'elpin'."

I couldn't help but smile at the irony of how this all worked out.

Alchemy of the Heart: Shavon Sun Cloud

Alchemy of the Heart: Shavon Sun Cloud

New Beginnings

I awoke with a start. I looked around the cottage. It was just Shavon and me. The fog slowly lifted from my brain. The ladies had all left yesterday after breakfast.

I had felt like a well-loved toy. I was hugged, kissed, and re-hugged many times as each person left the retreat. Apparently, there was no formal departure time. The process stretched out for many hours, which made it exceptionally hard for me. So many goodbyes. Correction, so many heartfelt goodbyes.

The hardest goodbye was when Caireann left. Tears unabashedly streamed down my face. In Caireann's special way, she said, "Oi won't be leavin' de country witout anoder visit or two. Shavahn still has tings to teach me!"

I quietly left the cottage, stoked the fire, and put the kettle on to boil. The water was just getting hot when Shavon came out of the cottage. She suggested, "Let's 'ave tea, clean up, and go get us a proper pub breakfast."

"Okay!"

It didn't take long to have the cottage and outside kitchen area stowed away because the thirty helping hands for the weekend insisted that we let them help clean up before they left. They did a mighty fine job of it!

I had carried the last load of things to the car when Shavon appeared at the car. "De cottage is locked, de car is loaded, and Oi'm starval. Let's go!"

I grinned and replied, "I am famished as well."

We hopped into the car and headed to the same pub that catered our pies for the weekend. After an over-the-top vegetable omelet, with orange juice and tea, we were more than full.

We were itching to get back home and rest, so Shavon quickly paid the bill for both the weekend and our meal today, and we were off. We made one quick stop at a bank to deposit a whole bunch of cash collected from the ladies at the weekend experience.

After we unloaded the car and put things into their proper places, I made us a cup of tea. I brought the tea out into the yard where Shavon was sitting. As I handed her a cup of tea I said, "Penny for your thoughts."

Shavon smiled, "De weekend went very lettle like Oi tought it would, but in a great way. Yahr presence was a good ting. 'Ow was the weekend for ye? Oi mean really, 'ow was it fahr ye?"

I chuckled, "Truthfully, had you told me I would be crying my eyes out in front of three ladies and thinking death has got to be

Alchemy of the Heart: Shavon Sun Cloud

less painful than what I went through, I probably would have run very, very far away. I might not have even come back.

The truth is, I didn't like the parts of me I saw. I was disgusted by my previous behaviors. Although I did like the glimpses of the potential of what I could be. I am liking the Devin that sings, the Devin that gives hugs, and the Devin that gets hugs.

So, yes, I am really glad I went." I chuckled and added, "But I was concerned about being with thirty naked women!"

Shavon giggled, "Oi tought dat might cause ye some concern."

I continued with my rambling, "Truth is, I am enjoying learning from you, and I am enjoying our time together. I am aware that I only have a couple more weeks with you here before I fly home. I am looking forward to learning what I can from you... and now from the entire circle."

We both watched as the mail truck drove up and placed a great deal of mail in the mailbox on the edge of the driveway.

Shavon smiled, "Oi've enjoyed our time together. Oi've enjoyed teachin' ye and Oi've enjoyed watchin' ye learn. Oi've enjoyed watchin' ye become de man ye were always destined to be."

Shavon stood up, "Let's get de mail. Dere looks to be a laht of it."

Alchemy of the Heart: Shavon Sun Cloud

I stood and we walked together to get the mail. It was a good thing we both went as there was more than one person could successfully carry.

We dropped the mail onto the table. Shavon continued her explanation while absent-mindedly going through her mail. "Devahn, when ye first arrived, Oi tought we would do a couple o' workshops and maybe a retreat. Never in me wildest imagination did Oi envision de depth and direction de retreat, or yahr trainin's would go. Oi never imagined how much ye would absorb as a student. Devahn, ye've done a fantastic job."

I was almost blushing. I rarely, if ever, received praise so, I didn't know how to properly handle it other than to be embarrassed by it.

Shavon continued with that same tone of voice I heard when I met her in Florida and she was scheming, "Devahn, Oi don't know what it looks like and ow it would work…"

She paused mid-sentence as she spied an envelope with air mail stickers all over it on the table. She tore open the envelope and almost ripped apart the letter trying to unfold it!

As she devoured the letter, I picked up the envelope. It was post-marked from Peru.

Excitedly, Shavon screeched, "Yes, Yes, YES!!!"

Alchemy of the Heart: Shavon Sun Cloud

She looked at me like a crazed woman and squealed with excitement, "Devahn, 'ow do ye feel about goin' to Peru wit me?"

Alchemy of the Heart: Shavon Sun Cloud

Alchemy of the Heart: Shavon Sun Cloud

Books also by L. Neil Thrussell

A Warrior's Heart: The Awakening

A Warrior's Heart: Perseverance

A Warrior's Heart: Convocation

A Warrior's Heart books series translated into Spanish

El Corazón de un Guerrero: El Despertar

El Corazón de un Guerrero: Perseverancia

El Corazón de un Guerrero: Convocatoria

Alchemy of the Heart: Shavon Sun Cloud

Alchemy of the Heart: Shavon Sun Cloud

Alchemy of the Heart shares the teaching of the Shin Dao: To learn more go to: www.shindao.com

The Four Pillars of the Shin Dao are:

Opening Hearts

Inspiring Minds

Developing Bodies

Elevating Spirits

"There is a magnet in your heart that will attract true friends. That magnet is unselfishness, thinking of others first… when you learn to live for others, they will live for you."

- Paramahansa Yogananda

Alchemy of the Heart: Shavon Sun Cloud

Alchemy of the Heart: Shavon Sun Cloud

About the Author

L. Neil Thrussell (1962 - present)

I have always loved to write and make up stories, but I was a closet writer until 2010. That's when I began to write seriously and let people see my work.

As an author I really don't like to be bound by facts or truth, so I love to write fiction, though I occasionally do write non-fiction. "The Relationship Survival Guide for Men: 7 Secrets Every Man Needs to Know About Women" is proof of my ability to write quality self-help material, but even my non-fiction is written with a lot of fun incorporated into it.

I was thrilled to have my dream of becoming an Amazon best-seller come true when the very first novel I self-published, "A Warrior's Heart: The Awakening" hit the best-seller list in 2012. That book was inspired by a recurring dream, and it seemed to write itself. Not long into the writing, I realized the story that came to me in a dream would be a trilogy.

The second book, "A Warrior's Heart: Perseverance" turned out a little differently than I expected, as once again the story seemed to write itself and take a slight detour from what I initially envisioned... Enjoy the surprise!

The final chapter in the A Warrior's Heart trilogy was the hardest one for me to write. I didn't want it to end. Seriously, I cried as I wrote the last lines! I loved the characters so much.

I started writing again in earnest in 2019, when I began writing 'Alchemy of the Heart: Shavon Sun Cloud' as well as a new genre for me a book in the action/mystery espionage genre.

Alchemy of the Heart: Shavon Sun Cloud

I recently retired for a fulfilling full-time career and now have the time to dedicate my time to writing. So you will see more works from me a faster output.

I trust you will and have enjoyed my books as much as I have enjoyed writing them.

Life is too short, get off the couch and pursue your dreams.

L. Neil Thrussell
www.neilthrussell.com

www.ingramcontent.com/pod-product-compliance
Lightning Source LLC
LaVergne TN
LVHW011415080426
835512LV00005B/71